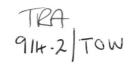 

TOWN WALKS

TOWN WALKS

MARSHALL CAVENDISH

From 1 April 1996, local authority boundaries in Scotland will change.
For up-to-date information, contact the relevant regional council
or the Scottish Office:

Dumfries & Galloway (01387) 61234
Borders (01835) 823301
Strathclyde (0141) 204 2900
Lothian (0131) 229 9292
Central (01786) 442000
Fife (01592) 754411
Scottish Office, Edinburgh (0131) 556 8400

This edition published in 1995 by
Marshall Cavendish Books, London
(a division of Marshall Cavendish Partworks Ltd)

Copyright © Marshall Cavendish 1995

ISBN 1 85435 836 7

British Library Cataloguing in Publication Data:
A catalogue record for this book is available from the British Library

Printed and bound in Spain

Some of this material has previously appeared in the Marshall Cavendish partwork OUT & ABOUT

CONTENTS

Foreword

The variety of towns and cities in Great Britain is as wide as that of the British countryside itself and just as enjoyable to walk through. Like landscapes, towns can be wild or tame, familiar or unusual, quiet or noisy, welcoming or forbidding, airy or confined, but never dull. There is always something of interest in them, whether architectural, historical or involving past inhabitants. Some towns are harmonious, built according to a plan and largely but never entirely of a unified design; others are a collision course of streets arguing with natural and manmade obstacles, and of clashing architectural styles.

For commerce or defence purposes, many towns are located on sites that would not ordinarily be recommended for development. Consequently, Great Britain has a fascinating assortment of hill towns. Some, such as Durham and Shrewsbury, are encircled by rivers; others, including Edinburgh and Montgomery, are dominated by their castles. Newcastle upon Tyne is a further example of a town which has developed with a dependence on the river for trade. In each, the solutions employed to erect buildings and lay streets on impossible gradients are fascinating to witness – and breathtaking to experience.

MARKET TOWNS

Most British towns developed as a result of people coming to them to trade their goods. Some later acquired additional functions that enriched or enlarged them as, for example, seats of academic learning; the rest depended on their markets and subsequently died when these ceased to exist. Today, most market towns hold markets on just one or two days a week, usually Saturday and one mid-week day. Try and visit on market day as the town will be immeasurably enlivened by the colourful awnings of the market stalls, the cheeky banter of the traders and the cornucopia of bargains and curiosities. Otherwise, you may be faced with a municipal car park in the centre of the town and be left to imagine the scene. One of the biggest and liveliest markets in England takes place in Norwich, where there has been a market since the eleventh century. Other market towns featured in *TOWN WALKS* include Totnes, where the owners of the houses in the market place extended their upper storeys to create what effectively became a covered arcade; Hexham, where the eighteenth-century Shambles are still in use; and Boston, which boasts a medieval Guildhall and Georgian Assembly Rooms as well as a covered market.

No market is of any use if goods cannot be brought there or taken away. For heavy goods of low unit value, such as coal, corn, iron and timber, transport by water was safest, cheapest and most reliable. Consequently, coastal towns such as Newcastle upon Tyne and Norwich, and towns along the inland waterways, such as Burton upon Trent, Shrewsbury and Wisbech, grew in importance during the seventeenth and eighteenth centuries as these commodities developed greater economic value during the Industrial Revolution.

SEASIDE RESORTS

Other towns grew in response to the nineteenth-century fashion for seaside resorts. Brighton had been popular since 1750 but, until the beginning of the nineteenth century, the area now known as Bournemouth was open heathland, from the southern edge of which deep valleys cut through the cliffs to the sea. An Enclosure Act in 1806 divided the heath among local landowners who then built large country homes and smaller cottages upon it. By 1835, a seaside resort of detached villas began to develop and today the town is a bustling mecca for holidaymakers all year round.

Although formerly an important market town, the city of Cambridge is famous today for its beautiful colleges, many of which back on to the River Cam. A seat of learning since the twelfth century, Cambridge boasts impressive examples of medieval, perpendicular and Tudor architecture. Most striking of all is King's College Chapel, easily visited by a short detour from the walk.

CATHEDRAL SKYLINE

Almost any approach to the city of Ely affords a breathtaking view of its impressive cathedral carved against the skyline. It is not difficult to imagine the impact this structure must have had on local people, especially those tending the fenland fields who would stop to pray the Angelus when the cathedral bells tolled. Across the Scottish border, the well-preserved medieval towns of St Andrews and Biggar enable the visitor to take several steps back in time, combining a wealth of architecture from medieval to Victorian with museums celebrating the towns' more recent attributes as the cradle of golf and the home of the Albion motor car respectively.

The towns of Alloway and Laugherne have themselves become well-known thanks to the fame of two respective residents and their writings. All over Alloway there are reminders that this was the childhood home of Scotland's most famous poet, Robert Burns, and, when walking along the cliffs of the Welsh seaside town of Laugherne, it is easy to appreciate the peace and solace the town must have brought to the troubled poet Dylan Thomas in the last four years of his life spent there.

CHARACTER AND STYLE

It is, of course, possible to walk through any town and enjoy it without knowing anything of the local history, but TOWN WALKS will reward the visitor who likes to do a little background reading on each of the different locations. As well as identifying the range of local architecture and other features relevant to each town from cathedrals to canals, TOWN WALKS gives a brief chronical of the events that shaped the development of the towns and details of well-known local personalities who have contributed to the towns' individual characters.

In addition, there is a wealth of up-to-date information on museums and places of specific interest. Together these facts combine to create a fascinating profile of each location and turn each walk into a true voyage of discovery.

Introduction to
TOWN WALKS

Walking has become one of the most popular pastimes in Britain. To enjoy walking, you don't need any special skills, you don't have to follow rules or join expensive clubs, and you don't need any special equipment – though a pair of walking boots is a good idea! It is an easy way of relaxing and getting some exercise, and of enjoying nature and the changing seasons.

TOWN WALKS *will give you ideas for walks in your own neighbourhood and in other areas of Britain. All the walks are devised to appeal to architectural enthusiasts and general walkers alike, and range in length from about 2 to 9 miles (3.25 to 14.5 km) and in difficulty from very easy to mildly strenuous. Whether circular or linear, the walks have been planned so that you will always be able to get back to your starting point.*

THE WALKS

Devised by experts and tested for accuracy, each walk is accompanied by clear instructions and an enlarged section of an Ordnance Survey map. The flavour of the walk and highlights to look out for are described in the introductory text. Feature boxes provide extra insight into items of local historical and environmental interest.

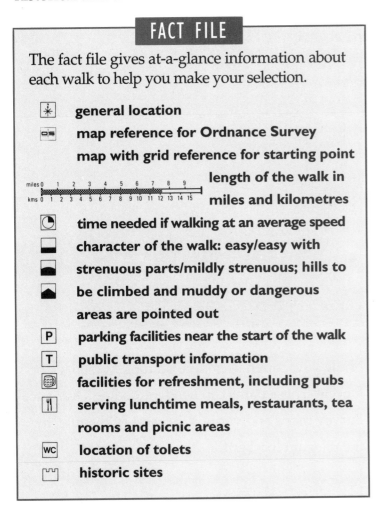

FACT FILE

The fact file gives at-a-glance information about each walk to help you make your selection.

☀ **general location**

os **map reference for Ordnance Survey map with grid reference for starting point**

length of the walk in

miles 0 1 2 3 4 5 6 7 8 9
kms 0 1 2 3 4 5 6 7 8 9 10 11 12 13 14 15

miles and kilometres

◐ **time needed if walking at an average speed**

▬ **character of the walk: easy/easy with**

◣ **strenuous parts/mildly strenuous; hills to**

▲ **be climbed and muddy or dangerous areas are pointed out**

P **parking facilities near the start of the walk**

T **public transport information**

▣ **facilities for refreshment, including pubs**

🍴 **serving lunchtime meals, restaurants, tea rooms and picnic areas**

WC **location of tolets**

▥ **historic sites**

ABOVE: *Colourful narrowboats are an attractive reminder of the days when the goods manufactured in towns and cities were transported to other parts of the country by inland waterways rather than by road.*

LOCAL HISTORY

TOWN WALKS relates the history of Britain's town centres; how changes in fashion combined with developments in building techniques to produce the urban landscape we have today. It also retells ancient legends, points out unusual architectural details and famous residents, past and present, and explains traditional crafts and industries.

DISCOVER NATURE

One of the greatest pleasures of going for a walk is the sense of being close to nature. On these walks, you can feel the wind, smell the pine trees, hear the birds and see the beauty of the countryside, as well as discover Britain's urban heritage.

You will become more aware of the seasons – the beginning of new life in the forests and fields, the bluebell carpets in spring woodlands, the dazzling beauty of rhododendron bushes in early summer, the swaying cornfields of summer, and the golden colours of leaves in autumn. TOWN WALKS tells you what to look out for and where to find it.

ORDNANCE SURVEY MAPS

All the walks in the TOWN WALKS are illustrated on large-scale, full-colour maps supplied by the Ordnance Survey which is justifiably proud of its worldwide reputation for excellence and accuracy. For extra clarity, the maps have been enlarged to a scale of 1:21,120 (3 inches to 1 mile).

The route for each walk is marked clearly on the map, together with numbered stages that relate to the walk directions and letters noting points of interest that are described in detail in the text.

RIGHTS OF WAY

Throughout the countryside there is a network of paths and byways. Most are designated 'rights of way': footpaths, open only to people on foot, and

RIGHT: *The picturesque village of Widecombe in the heart of Dartmoor makes a beautiful setting for the annual fair.*

BELOW: *Brown hares boxing in spring.*

bridleways, open to people on foot, horseback or bicycle. These paths can be identified on Ordnance Survey maps and verified, in cases of dispute, by the relevant local authority.

THE LAW OF TRESPASS

If you find a public right of way barred to you, you may remove the obstruction or take a short detour around it. However, in England and Wales, if you stray from the footpath you are trespassing and could be sued in a civil court for damages. In Scotland, rights of way are not recorded on definitive maps, nor is there a law of trespass. Although you may cross mountain and moorland paths,

THE COUNTRY CODE

- Enjoy the countryside, and respect its life and work
- Always guard against risk of fire
- Fasten all gates
- Keep your dogs under close control
- Keep to public footpaths across farmland
- Use gates and stiles to cross fences, hedges and walls
- Leave livestock, crops and machinery alone
- Take your litter home
- Help to keep all water clean
- Protect wildlife, plants and trees
- Take special care on country roads
- Make no unnecessary noise

landowners are permitted to impose restrictions on access, which should be obeyed.

ABOVE RIGHT: *Carelessness with cigarettes, matches or camp fires can be devastating in a forest, especially during a period of drought.*

COMMONS AND PARKS

Walkers are generally able to wander freely on most commons and beaches in England and Wales. There are also country parks, set up by local authorities for public recreation – parkland, woodland, heath or farmland.

Most regions of great scenic beauty in England and Wales are designated National Parks or Areas of Outstanding Natural Beauty (AONB). In Scotland, they are known as National Scenic Areas (NSAs)

or AONBs. Most of this land is privately owned and there is no right of public access although local authorities may have negotiated access agreements.

CONSERVATION

National park, AONB or NSA status is intended to protect the landscape, guarding against unsuitable development while encouraging enjoyment of its beauty. Nature reserves are areas which are set aside for conservation. Although some offer public access, most require permission to enter.

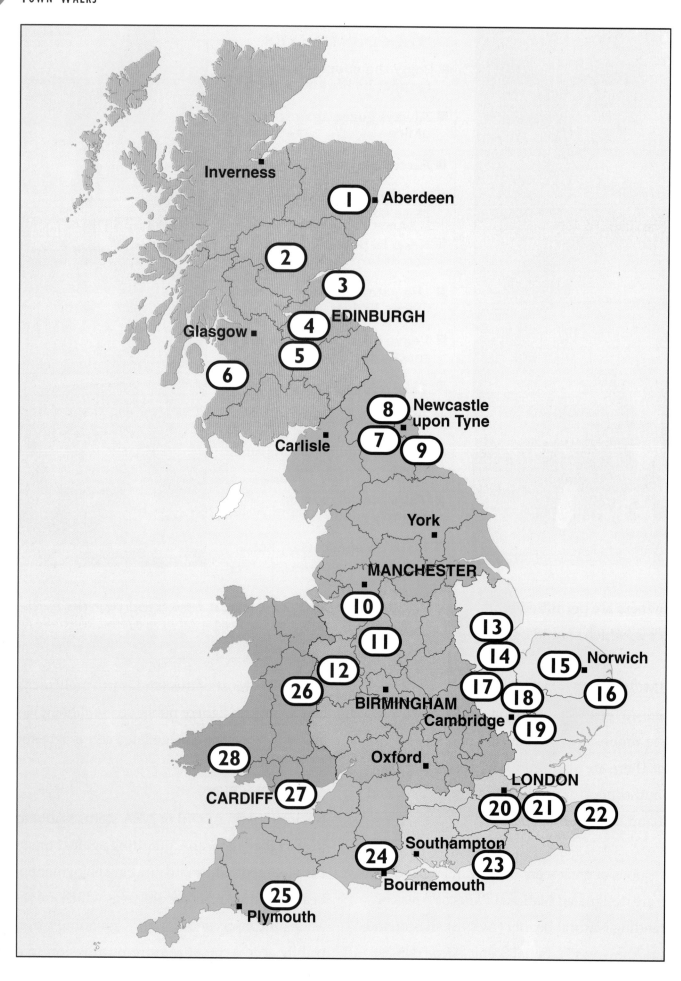

Town Walks

All the walks featured in this book are plotted and numbered on the map opposite and listed in the box below.

1 **The Granite City**

2 **Gateway to the Highlands**

3 **A Royal and Ancient Town**

4 **Hidden Edinburgh**

5 **The Little Town of Biggar**

6 **Burns' Homeland**

7 **Historic Hexham**

8 **Old Newcastle**

9 **The Proud Towers**

10 **At the Base of the Pennines**

11 **Going for a Burton**

12 **By Dogpole and Grope Lane**

13 **On the Stump**

14 **A Fenland Isle**

15 **Norwich City**

16 **The Far East**

17 **On the Brinks**

18 **Ship of the Fens**

19 **Light Blue Colleges**

20 **Hills of Croydon**

21 **A Royal Park**

22 **Triple-Decker Sandwich**

23 **Backstreet Brighton**

24 **Secret Bournemouth**

25 **From a Quay to a Castle**

26 **An Ancient Border Town**

27 **Waves Across the Waves**

28 **The Poet and the Castles**

*E*arth has not anything to show more fair;
Dull would he be of soul who could pass by
A sight so touching in its majesty:
This City now doth, like a garment, wear
The beauty of the morning; silent, bare,
Ships, towers, domes, theatres, and temples lie
Open unto the fields, and to the sky;
All bright and glittering in the smokeless air.

Composed upon Westminster Bridge
William Wordsworth

USING MAPS

Although TOWN WALKS gives you all the information you need, it is useful to have some basic map skills.

A large-scale map is the answer to identifying where you are. Britain is fortunate in having the best mapping agency in the world, the Ordnance Survey, which produces high-quality maps, the most popular being the 1:50,000 Landranger series. However, the most useful for walkers are the 1:25,000 Pathfinder, Explorer and Outdoor Leisure maps.

THE LIE OF THE LAND

A map provides more than just a bird's eye view of the land, it also conveys information about the terrain; it distinguishes between foot-paths and bridleways and shows boundaries.

Symbols are used to identify a variety of land-marks such as churches, stations, castles and caves. The shape of the land is indicated by con-tour lines. Each line represents land at a specific height so it is possible to read the gradient from the spacing of the lines.

GRID REFERENCES

All Ordnance Survey maps are over-printed with a framework of squares known as the National Grid. This is a reference system which, by breaking the country down into squares, allows you to pinpoint any place in the country and give it a unique reference number; very useful when making rendezvous arrangements. On OS Landranger, Pathfinder and Outdoor Leisure maps it is possible to give a reference to an accuarcy of 100 metres. Grid squares on these maps cover an area of 1 km x 1 km on the ground.

GIVING A GRID REFERENCE

Blenheim Palace in Oxfordshire has a grid reference of **SP 441 161**. This is constructed as follows:

SP These letters identify the 100 km grid square in which Blenheim Palace lies. These squares form the basis of the National Grid. Information on the 100 km square covering a particular map is always given in the map key.

441 161 This six figure reference locates the position of Blenheim Palace to 100 metres in the 100 km grid square.

44 This part of the reference is the number of the grid line which forms the western (left-hand) boundary of the 1 km grid square in which Blenheim Palace appears. This number is printed in the top and bottom margins of the relevant OS map (Pathfinder 1092 in this case).

16 This part of the reference is the number of the grid line which forms the southern (lower) boundary of the 1 km grid square in which Blenheim Palace appears. This number is printed in the left- and right-hand margins of the relevant OS map (Pathfinder 1092).

These two numbers together (SP 4416) locate the bottom left-hand corner of the 1 km grid square in which Blenheim Palace appears. The remaining figures in the reference **441 161** pinpoint the position within that square by dividing its western boundary lines into tenths and estimating on which imaginary tenths line Blenheim Palace lies.

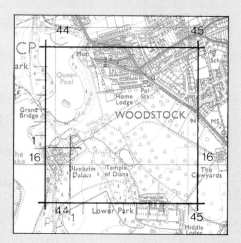

THE GRANITE CITY

EDINBURGH PHOTOGRAPHIC LIBRARY. INSET: MELVIN GREY/NHPA

From Old Aberdeen to the golden sands of Aberdeen beach

▲*Aberdeen is a bustling city, but its industrial areas do not encroach on its wide, unspoilt beach. A male long-tailed duck (right) in winter plumage. Its song has been likened to the sound of bagpipes.*

This walk leads you through Aberdeen's history. It starts and finishes within the campus of Aberdeen University, in the area known as Old Aberdeen, which has narrow cobbled streets, ancient churches, St Machar's Cathedral, narrow alleys and a quiet and peaceful atmosphere of scholarly life.

The City of Aberdeen is, thanks to the recent exploration of the North Sea oil fields, a prosperous place. Its position in the extreme north-east of Scotland has meant that it was a centre for North Sea fishing in the past, but the new ocean resource of oil has tempted many away from this traditional industry. Nowadays, the harbour, which once resounded to the cry of the 'fisher wifies' as they gutted the

FACT FILE

☀	Aberdeen
◻	Pathfinder 246 (NJ 80/90), grid reference NJ 939079

miles 0 1 2 3 4 5 6 7 8 9 10 miles
kms 0 1 2 3 4 5 6 7 8 9 10 11 12 13 14 15 kms

◔	Allow 2½ hours
▬	Cobbled roads, tarmac, footpaths and beach
P	At Aberdeen University
☗	Cafés, tea rooms and restaurants in Aberdeen. Pub and hotels at Bridge of Don
WC	Public toilets beside beach

herring, is full of oil supply vessels.

But not all is new. Old Aberdeen still attracts tourists from around the world and the city still boasts some of the finest granite structures in the world.

A UNIVERSITY TOWN

The university was founded in 1494-5 by Bishop Elphinstone, who founded it within the King's College **Ⓐ**. The college has an open lantern in the form of the Imperial crown surmounting its tower. The chapel is a fine example of the style called Scottish Flamboyant Gothic. Opposite the college stands the oriental-style gateway of Powis House.

Close by King's College is the ancient St Machar's Cathedral **Ⓑ**.

THE WALK

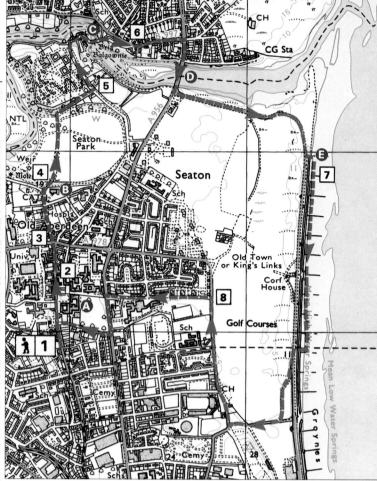

OLD ABERDEEN

The walk begins near King's College **Ⓐ**, *in the cobbled street known as College Bounds, close to its junction with University Road.*

1 Wander through King's College and return to College Bounds. The Powis House Gate is immediately across the road.

2 Turn right and follow the road past the New King's College. Continue past the cottages, now used by the university professors.

3 Continue past the library, across St Machar's Drive, and continue along The Chanonry, past the entrance to Aberdeen's Botanic Gardens. Continue to St Machar's Cathedral **Ⓑ** ahead.

4 Leave the cathedral grounds by the north gate and turn immediately right. Go downhill to a footpath, which crosses Seaton Park.

At the north end of the park climb some steps and follow the path to the right until you come to a public road.

5 Turn left and follow this road with the Hillhead of Seaton Halls of Residence on your left. Follow the road to the Brig O'Balgownie **Ⓒ**. Cross the road to the bridge, pass the fishermen's cottages and walk to Balgownie Road.

6 Follow Balgownie Road right until you come to Bridge of Don Road. Turn right, cross the Bridge of Don **Ⓓ** and immediately turn left to follow the road alongside the River Don to the beach **Ⓔ**.

7 Walk along the beach for 1 mile (1.6 km), then climb up onto the promenade. Across the promenade a slip road leads down beside a putting green. Take this and follow it to Golf Road, then turn right. Continue on this

road around the southern extremity of the golf course to Pittodrie Stadium, the home of Aberdeen Football Club.

8 Leave Golf Road by turning left into Regent

Walk. Follow this street to its junction with King Street. Turn left and follow King Street and turn right to University Road. Follow this back to College Bounds.

◀*The Brig O'Balgownie, a 14th-century bridge with a single Gothic arch, spans salmon pools where hundreds of salmon can be seen migrating upstream.*

The present building stands on the site of an even more ancient holy structure, said to have been erected in AD 581 by St Machar himself.

Marischal College is an impressive piece of granite architecture with a magnificent pinnacled façade. Near it is Provost Skene's House, which was built in 1545, but bears the name of Provost Skene who lived there in the 17th century. This turreted building is now a museum with several rooms beautifully furnished in Georgian, Regency and Victorian styles.

At Schoolhill stands St Nicholas' Church, at one time the largest parish church in Scotland. Behind the defiant statue of Sir William Wallace stands Her Majesty's Theatre. Union Terrace runs beside

landscaped gardens and leads to Aberdeen's main thoroughfare, Union Street, with a 19th-century music hall, the magnificent cathedral and St John's Church.

BRIG O'BALGOWNIE

Just north of St Machar's Cathedral, across Seaton Park, the old Brig O'Balgownie **Ⓒ** crosses the River Don. A strange legend is attached to the Brig. It is claimed that when 'a wife's ae son, and a mear's ae foal' crosses the bridge, it will collapse. So first-born sons should take care not to cross the Brig O'Balgownie on a first-born foal, or there could be trouble!

Another bridge, the Bridge of Don **Ⓓ** is much younger than the Brig O'Balgownie. It is situated near the mouth of the River Don, where Aberdeen's magnificent beach **Ⓔ** stretches for miles. The beach offers fine bathing, albeit in the cold waters of the North Sea.

A short stroll around one of Scotland's most historic towns

The small whitewashed town of Dunkeld is one of the gems of Perthshire and is also one of the most important places in the history of Scotland. It lies in a beautiful setting beside the River Tay, with wooded hills and crags towering around the town.

Several places have been styled the 'Gateway to the Highlands'. Dunkeld probably has the strongest claim to the title, as it straddles the 'Highland Line', the southern edge of the Grampian Mountains which was once the historical meeting point of Highland and Lowland cultures. In 1689, friction between the two led to the Clash of Arms, when Dunkeld was burnt to the ground after the Battle of Killiecrankie.

Much of the centre of the town was rebuilt after the destruction of 1689, and was restored by the National Trust for Scotland in the

Dunkeld sits proudly above the River Tay, surrounded by woodland. The ladybird (inset), which is a kind of beetle, is found all over Britain. The seven-spot variety is the most common.

AA PHOTO LIBRARY. INSET: ANDREW J. PURCELL/BRUCE COLEMAN LTD

FACT FILE

✳	Dunkeld, 12 miles (19km) north of Perth
🗺	Pathfinder 324 NO 04/14, grid reference NO 025426

miles 0 1 2 3 4 5 6 7 8 9 10 miles
kms 0 1 2 3 4 5 6 7 8 9 10 11 12 13 14 15 kms

🕐	Allow 1 hour
	Street pavements and good paths. One short ascent up steep steps, which can be avoided
P	In town centre streets or in car park at north end of Atholl Street
T	Regular bus and train services to and from Dunkeld
🍴	Numerous pubs, restaurants and cafés
WC	Near Visitor Centre and by car park

1950s. There is a fine cathedral in a magnificent situation on the north shore of the Tay, not far from the great bridge built by Telford in 1809.

The walk starts at the Tourist Association Visitor Centre **A**, where street maps are available, as well as detailed information about Dunkeld and the surrounding area. There are interesting buildings all around the square, dating from the late 17th and early 18th centuries.

From the Visitor Centre, the walk passes the fountain and crosses the square to the Ell Shop **B**, the building on the corner of Cathedral Street. Built as a hospital in 1753, this is a now a National Trust shop. It takes its name from the 'ell', a weaver's measure; one is on the wall at the corner of the old market.

CENTRE OF WORSHIP

In Cathedral Street, the whitewashed houses have colourful displays of flowers in their windows and doorways in season. At the far end is the Rectory, the oldest house in Dunkeld. It is by the gates to the cathedral **C**, which stands in an idyllic setting among tree-shaded lawns on the banks of the Tay. There were Christian settlements in Dunkeld as early as the 6th century.

THE WALK

DUNKELD

The walk starts at the Visitor Centre **A**.

1 ➤ Cross the square to the Ell Shop **B** on the opposite corner. Turn right and walk to the gates at the end of Cathedral Street. Explore the cathedral **C** and its grounds beside the Tay. Follow the path clockwise around the cathedral, with fine views of the wooded hills to the north of Dunkeld, and return, via a tour of the grounds, to the cathedral gates.

2 ➤ Turn right out of the gates and follow a path beside a high stone wall, which leads to the river **D**. At the riverside, turn left along a grassy path leading towards Dunkeld Bridge **E**, which is now clearly visible. Pass under an arch of the

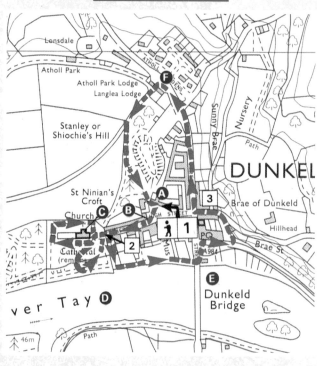

bridge, then turn left towards the Atholl Arms Hotel and turn right at the road. Pass the Taybank

Hotel. A few paces beyond, take the steep steps up to the left to reach Sundial House and Brae Street.

Turn left down Brae Street to the crossroads of High Street, Bridge Street and Atholl Street. (Those wishing to avoid the steep steps should join Bridge Street at the corner of the Atholl Arms Hotel and follow it to the crossroads at the bottom of Brae Street.)

3 ➤ Follow Atholl Street to the edge of the town. After passing the car park on the left, follow the road round to Dunkeld Lodge **F**. Turn left through the archway and follow a narrow road for a little way. Turn left just after a lay-by, through a gap in the fence. Follow a path beside Stanley Hill, which is on your right. At a fork in the path, by some picnic tables, go left. Soon you pass through an archway and arrive back at the Visitor Centre.

An abbey was founded here in AD 815. In AD 844, Dunkeld became, with Scone, one of the twin capitals of the united kingdoms of the Picts and the Scots.

The Danes plundered the town several times, but Dunkeld continued to be a major religious centre, becoming a bishopric in 1127. The cathedral was built between 1308 and 1501, but most of it was ruined during the Reformation. The chancel was later restored and now serves as the parish church.

As you return to the cathedral gates, a path leads down to the Tay **D** where a riverside path continues towards Dunkeld Bridge **E**, one of the finest achievements of the great engineer, Thomas Telford.

RECORD SALMON

The Tay is famous as one of the world's best salmon rivers. The British record salmon, weighing 64lb (29kg), was caught just downstream from Dunkeld in 1922.

Passing under the bridge, the route returns to the town centre via steps leading to Sundial House and Brae Street. From here, there are fine views over the High Street and the houses in front of the cathedral.

◀ *Though traces of the original 12th-century Dunkeld Cathedral remain, most of it is 14th- and 15th-century.*

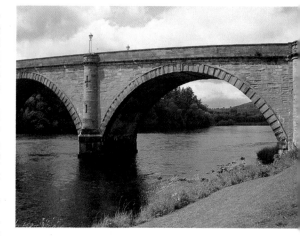

▲ *The impressive Dunkeld Bridge was designed by Scottish engineer Thomas Telford and constructed in 1809.*

Turning into Atholl Street, the walk passes through the main shopping area of Dunkeld, where several interesting shops and galleries sell local craft products. At the edge of the town, the route passes under the archway of Dunkeld Lodge **F** and continues around Stanley Hill, through attractive parkland, before returning to the town centre.

K. KEANE/SCOTLAND IN FOCUS. INSET: DAVID OVERGASH/BRUCE COLEMAN LTD

▲*The remains of the fortified castle of St Andrews dominate the town. Its commanding position helped guard the bay and countryside. Daisies (left) grow in short grassland nearby.*

From the home of golf to Scotland's oldest university

St Andrews is beautifully situated in a sheltered bay on the coast of Fife. It is a town of great character and exceptional historic interest. From at least the 6th century it was a stronghold of the Pictish kings and the site of an influential monastery of the Celtic Church. In the 8th century it became a centre for the pilgrims who came to worship the remains of St Andrew,

Scotland's patron saint. The cathedral and the castle were founded in the 12th century, and Scotland's oldest university was founded at St Andrews in 1410.

Today, St Andrews is world-famous as a golfing centre, while the heart of the town has an order and dignity matched by few of the remaining medieval cities of north-western Europe. The walk explores the heart of the town, its main historical buildings and the famous golf course.

The walk starts at the car park overlooking the great sweep of West Sands Ⓐ, a superb beach stirringly

---

FACT FILE

⁎ St Andrews, 11 miles (18 km) south-east of Dundee

O/S Pathfinder 363 (NO 41/51), grid reference NO 505172

miles 0 1 2 3 4 5 6 7 8 9 10 miles
kms 0 1 2 3 4 5 6 7 8 9 10 11 12 13 14 15 kms

◑ Allow 2 to 3 hours

▭ Pavements, good paths and a sandy beach

P Large car park at start of walk

T Regular buses and trains

🍴 All facilities in town

WC At car park

⌂ Cathedral Museum open all year. British Golf Museum, Tel. (01334) 478880 for details

THE WALK

ST ANDREWS

The walk begins at the car park serving the British Golf Museum, opposite the Royal and Ancient Golf Club. To reach it by car, follow signs for West Sands **A**.

➡ Turn left out of the car park, passing the British Golf Museum **B** on the left and the Royal and Ancient Golf Club **C** on the right. Continue up Golf Place and turn left into North Street. Continue for just over ¼ mile (400 metres) to St Salvator's **D**. Enter the quadrangle through an archway and exit through a gateway on the left side of the quadrangle. Turn right down Butts Wynd. Continue to The Scores and turn right. Follow The Scores to the castle **E**. Continue along the road until it becomes a footpath that follows the cliff top. Enter the cathedral and priory grounds **F** through a gate in the precinct wall. After exploring the grounds and climbing St Rule's Tower, return to the footpath. Follow it down the hill to the

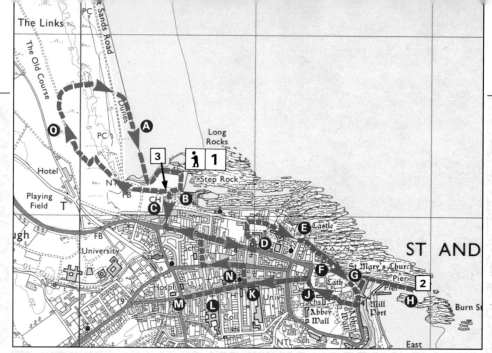

harbour, passing the remains of the Church of St Mary of the Rock **G**.

➡ Walk to the end of the pier **H** then return to the harbour. Follow it round to its southern end then take a right turn up The Pends **J**, which follows the south side of the cathedral wall and finally passes through an archway. Turn left into South Street and follow this to St Mary's College **K**, Blackfriars Chapel **L** and West Port **M**. Return on the other side of South Street and turn left along Church Street, the site of Holy Trinity Church **N**. Follow Church Street to Market Street, then turn

left and follow Market Street to Greyfriars Gardens. Turn right and continue to North Street. Turn left along North Street and then turn into Golf Place and arrive back at the Royal and Ancient Golf Club.

➡ Turn left opposite the British Golf Museum and follow a good path for a little over ¼ mile (400 metres), with the Old Course **O** on the left, until you reach the grass at the start of the New Course, with the starter building on the right. Just before the 'New Course' signboard, go left through a gap in the gorse bushes onto the Old

Course and turn right along a grassy and sandy path between the Old and New Courses. At one stage the path becomes rather indistinct, but keep straight on and it soon becomes a good gravel track. Turn right at a fork and cross the New and the Jubilee Courses (low-flying golf balls are a hazard) and follow the track to some low buildings. Beyond is another fairway. Cross it to a car park area and West Sands Road. Go over the road and the dunes and you will emerge on West Sands. Turn right along the beach and walk back to the car park.

▼*The beach at West Sands, where the walk ends, was where the runners trained in the film* **Chariots of Fire**.

depicted in the film *Chariots of Fire*. Near the beach is the British Golf Museum **B**, opposite the famous Royal and Ancient Golf Club **C**. Beyond the 'R & A' is the famous Old Course, where the Open Golf Championship is sometimes played.

THE UNIVERSITY

At the corner of Golf Place and North Street, the walk turns left into North Street and heads towards the centre of the old town. The main streets of St Andrews are wide and spacious with attractive, well-proportioned stone buildings. The main university buildings lie halfway along North Street on the left-hand side; the ruins of the cathedral are visible at the far end of the street.

Founded in 1410, the university

comprised the colleges of St Salvator's **D** (1450), St Leonard's (1512) and St Mary's (1537). St Salvator's and St Leonard's were amalgamated in 1747 to form United College. The entrance to St Salvator's is through an archway with heavy wooden doors that lead to a large quadrangle with well-kept lawns. Initials on the pavement in front of the archway mark the spot where Patrick Hamilton was burned at the stake in 1528 for teaching Lutheran doctrines. He was the first martyr of the Scottish Reformation. There is a superstition among students today that to set foot on the initials will mean doing badly in university examinations.

A gate exits from the spacious quadrangle into Butts Wynd, a

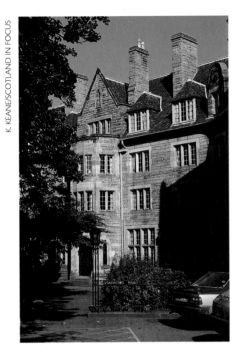

▲ *St Salvator's is one of the three original university colleges. The university was founded in 1410.*

narrow street leading to The Scores, a quiet road shaded by trees, with many university departments in the buildings on either side.

THE CASTLE

Soon the castle ❸ is reached. It dates from about 1200 and was at one time the principal residence of the Bishops of St Andrews. Protected on its north and east sides by high cliffs and the sea, it was once a formidable fortress and prison. The fascinating mine and counter-mine are a rare example of medieval siege technique, and the castle is also famous for its bottle dungeon, hollowed out of solid rock.

From here the walk follows the cliff top towards the grounds of the cathedral ❻, which are entered by a small gateway in the precinct wall. The cathedral was founded in 1160, while the ancient priory here dates from the 13th century. Despite the destructive efforts of the Reformation, the remains of the cathedral still give a vivid impression of the massive scale of what was once the largest church in the whole of Scotland.

ST RULE'S TOWER

In the grounds there is a visitor centre, where tickets are available for the museum and an ascent of St Rule's Tower. The museum has a collection of Celtic and medieval artefacts, including a superb sarcophagus that dates from the 8th or 10th century. Legend maintains that St Rule (also known as St Regulus) brought the relics of St Andrew to Fife. A church was built about 1130, but today only the choir and the tower remain. A steep ascent by spiral steps leads to the top of the 108-foot (33-metre) tower, from which there is a magnificent view over St Andrews and the surrounding coast and hills.

Returning to the cliff path, the route descends towards the harbour, passing the Church of St Mary of the Rock ❼. Only the foundations now remain of this Celtic settlement, which was perched on the cliff above the harbour. It fell into disuse as the Church of St Rule and the cathedral prospered.

During term-time, the harbour is the site of a colourful tradition after the Sunday morning service at St Salvator's Chapel, as the students embark on their customary walk

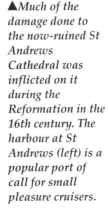

▲ *Much of the damage done to the now-ruined St Andrews Cathedral was inflicted on it during the Reformation in the 16th century. The harbour at St Andrews (left) is a popular port of call for small pleasure cruisers.*

along the pier ❽, wearing red gowns. The pier was constructed with stones from the ruins of the castle and the cathedral.

Leaving the harbour, the route returns to the town centre by following Pends Road beside the old wall of the cathedral. The wall is about 1 mile (1.6 km) long and was mainly built in the early 16th century. At the top, the road passes through The Pends ❿, a 14th-century vaulted gatehouse that formed the main entrance to the priory.

BOTH PHOTOS PETER DAVENPORT/EDINBURGH PHOTO LIBRARY

▲ *The greystone buildings of St Andrews give way to the open spaces of the golf links and the coast.*

From The Pends, South Street leads through the town to West Port, the main entrance to the old town of St Andrews, with several interesting buildings on the way. Just around the corner from The Pends is Queen Mary's House, a 16th-century house where Mary Queen of Scots is reputed to have stayed. Halfway along South Street is St Mary's College **K**, founded in 1537. It now houses the Faculty of Divinity. As you enter the quadrangle of St Mary's, there is a striking view of a magnificent holm oak, which was planted in 1728.

TOWN CENTRE

A little further along is the tourist information office and the town hall, which was built in 1858. Continuing towards West Port, there are the remains of Blackfriars Chapel **L**. All that is left of this small Dominican church is a spectacular single apse.

The West Port **M**, at the west end of South Street, is one of the few surviving city gates in Scotland. It

was built in 1580 and still serves as a thoroughfare. From here the walk crosses to the other side of South Street, which forms, with Market Street, the main shopping area of St Andrews. Reaching Church Street, there is the Holy Trinity Church **N**, which is the town kirk, dating from 1410. Church Street leads to the focal point of Market Street, the Mercat Cross, the original cross now replaced by a fountain.

GOLF LINKS

Soon you return to the Old Course **O**, and its first tee just in front of the 'R & A'. A westward path heads over the 500 acres (200 hectares) of golf links that lie to the north-west of St Andrews. About ½ mile (800 metres) along this path, a track eastwards crosses the New Course and the Jubilee Course to West Sands Road. Beyond the road, small sand dunes back the huge expanse of West Sands. The last section of the walk is along the beach, heading southwards towards the town of St Andrews and the car park.

The Home of Golf

Golf has been played in Fife since the 15th century or even earlier. In 1457 James II, King of Scots, banned the game so men would concentrate on their archery practice. Later, in 1567, Mary Queen of Scots played here. Today, St Andrews is internationally famous as the traditional home of this long-established sport.

The Royal and Ancient Golf Club was founded in 1754, acquiring its royal title in 1834 when King William IV was nominated as patron of the club. The clubhouse dates from 1854 and is recognized as the headquarters of world golf. Nearby is the British Golf Museum.

There are 15 golf courses in north-east Fife, including the legendary Old Course at St Andrews. This has been the site of 24 Open Championships, as well as many other professional and amateur events, including the Ryder Cup played between teams from Europe

and the USA. With a par of 72, the 6,566 yards (5,995 metres) are a great test for any golfer, especially on a windy day. The nearby New Course was laid out in 1895, two years before the Jubilee Course, which commemorates the 60th year of Queen Victoria's reign.

To the cheers of the crowd, many great golfers have strode across this bridge on their way to the 18th green and victory.

HIDDEN EDINBURGH

SCOTLAND

GLYN SATTERLEY.INSET:STEPHEN DALTON/NHPA

▲ *Whereas once it was a busy link between Edinburgh and Glasgow, the Union Canal is now a peaceful place. The swallow (left) rarely alights on the ground and drinks on the wing.*

A country walk by canal, river and old railway in the heart of Edinburgh

The Water of Leith **Ⓐ** flows from the Pentland Hills of the Firth of Forth through central Edinburgh. Its walkway forms one of the finest riverside walks in the country. Especially beautiful are the woodland sections, where the river runs through Craiglockhart Dell **Ⓑ**, and the Gorge of Colinton Dell **Ⓔ**. The mostly planted woods exhibit a tremendous variety of trees. In early summer, the smell of wild garlic here can be intoxicating. In former days, the river's power was used to drive water mills such as those at Redhall and beside Spylaw House **Ⓗ**. The weir and lade (mill-stream) that supplied water to Redhall Mill **Ⓓ** can still be seen and there are other weirs above Spylaw House and at Slateford **Ⓒ**.

RURAL COMMUNITY

Colinton **Ⓖ**, whose name means 'the village in the wood', was originally an isolated rural community that grew up around the head of Colinton Dell at a place that was easily forded by herdsmen and other travellers. It is now part of the city of Edinburgh, but has retained an authentic village quality with a

FACT FILE

- ✳ 2 miles (3.2 km) south-west of centre of Edinburgh on A70

- Pathfinders 420 (NT 26/36) and 407 (NT 26/37), grid reference NT 221707

  miles 0 1 2 3 4 5 6 7 8 9 10 miles
  kms 0 1 2 3 4 5 6 7 8 9 10 11 12 13 14 15 kms

- ◔ 2 hours

- On mostly excellent paths by canal, river and disused railway line

- P At start of walk at the Tickled Trout Inn or in nearby side streets

- T Numerous buses from the centre of Edinburgh

- ⍟ The Tickled Trout Inn at start of walk and the Royal Scot Inn in Colinton village — both have bar food.

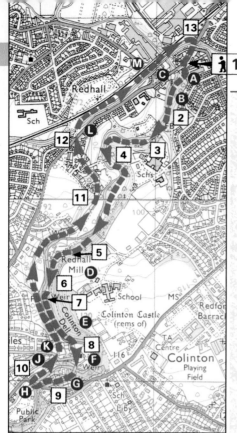

COLINTON

The walk begins at the Tickled Trout Inn on Lanark Road.

1 Take the dirt track that leaves the roadside left of the inn and curves behind it. Beside the Water of Leith **Ⓐ** it becomes a woodland path through Craiglockhart Dell **Ⓑ**. Immediately beyond the inn, the broken-down Slateford weir **Ⓒ** can be viewed by a short detour to the riverbank.

2 Soon a pipeline that bridges the river is reached and immediately afterwards the path forks. Keep right on the riverside path and follow it across a small stream (bridge) beside which is an old dome-

THE WALK

shaped stone shelter. On the far side of the stream the path rises and falls to negotiate some riverside rocks then passes a footbridge over the Water of Leith. Pause to view the river from the bridge but do not cross; keep to the near side.

3 At another fork, keep right down some wooden steps to follow the main path across a riverside meadow.

4 At a single-arched stone bridge, where there are some picnic tables, do not cross the river but keep straight on. The well-constructed path continues its meandering way along the near riverbank amongst trees and across meadows.

5 The path joins a dirt track at yet another bridge over the Water of Leith. Again do not cross the river, but keep straight on between some houses to reach the end of a tarmac road. The building at the water's edge here is Redhall Mill **Ⓓ**.

6 Turn right at the road to follow a dirt track that soon becomes a path. The path descends steps, crosses the lade (mill-stream) that formerly fed Redhall Mill and turns left to form a fine route between the lade and the river.

7 Soon you reach the weir that feeds the lade. You finally cross the river at a wooden bridge in the heart of Colinton Dell **Ⓔ**. On the far side of the bridge keep left and, avoiding all paths that branch to the right, stay beside the river until the path leads you to the foot of a flight of steps. Climb the steps to emerge onto a tarmac road beside the grounds of Colinton parish church.

8 Keep to the road as it joins Spylaw Bank Road and passes the iron gates at the church **Ⓕ** entrance. Once past the church, the road bears right, crosses a bridge over the Water of Leith and climbs into Colinton village **Ⓖ** at Spylaw Street. The Royal Scot Inn is on the right near the top.

9 A few paces beyond the inn, iron gates on the right mark the entrance to Spylaw Park and a sign reads 'Spylaw House'. Take the dirt track that descends from here to the Water of Leith, passing under a high, multi-arched road bridge, then crossing the river at a concrete bridge to enter Spylaw Park. Spylaw House **Ⓗ** stands beside the river. There is a children's playground in the far corner of the park.

10 On the far side of the bridge, turn right in front of a small stone building then climb the steps beside it to reach the disused railway line **Ⓙ** above. Turn right under the arch of the bridge to follow the line of the old railway through Easter Hailes Gate tunnel **Ⓚ** and along a level route high above the Water of Leith back towards the starting point of the walk.

11 At a fork about ½ mile (800 metres) beyond the tunnel keep left, then continue to keep left as the line veers away from the Water of Leith to pass under a small bridge and reach Lanark Road.

12 Two consecutive bridges carry the line across Lanark Road and the Union Canal **Ⓛ**. Once over the canal bridge, turn right down some steps to join the canal towpath then left along it. The canal soon crosses Slateford aqueduct **Ⓜ** and bears right to cross Slateford Road.

13 On the nearside of the Slateford bridge, a flight of wooden steps leads down to the roadside. Descend the steps and turn right at the bottom. The Tickled Trout Inn lies a few hundred paces up the road, which can be crossed at traffic lights beneath the canal bridge.

◀This mortsafe was hired out to prevent 'body-snatchers' from exhuming cadavers to sell to anatomy classes.

variety of buildings spanning the past four centuries. The parish church **Ⓕ**, rebuilt in 1909, stands on the site of a church dating back at least to the 11th century.

Further on is the point where an off-shoot of the Edinburgh-Glasgow railway reached Colinton in 1874. The line **Ⓙ** was closed in 1967 and now forms a fine walking route through Colinton Dell. The eerie Easter Hailes Gate tunnel **Ⓚ** is a long, curving and dimly-lit structure, with an uneven surface and a constantly dripping roof.

Soon after, you come to the Union Canal **Ⓛ**. The Colinton area has one of its finest stretches, with a 600-foot (183-metre), eight-arched aqueduct **Ⓜ** that gives fine views over the city.

GLYN SATTERLEY

A stroll around a country town that is full of surprises

Probably nowhere in Scotland has so much of interest in one place as the little town of Biggar on the border of Clydesdale with Tweeddale. To make the walking as well as the seeing worthwhile, the route makes a circuit outside the town to take in some fine high-level views over the surrounding countryside and hills.

MEDIEVAL TOWN

Biggar is a medieval town that was created a free Burgh of Barony by James II in 1451 as a mark of favour to the local landowner, Lord Fleming. The town retains its

▶ *Cadger's Brig is thought to have been crossed by William Wallace in the 12th century, while he was spying on the English army. Selfheal (inset) grows in the grassland around Biggar.*

JOHN WATNEY. INSET: G.CAMBRIDGE/NHPA

FACT FILE

- ✳ Biggar, 25 miles (40km) south-west of Edinburgh

- ⌗ Pathfinder 459 (NT 03/13), grid reference NT 038376

  miles 0 1 2 3 4 5 6 7 8 9 10 miles
  kms 0 1 2 3 4 5 6 7 8 9 10 11 12 13 14 15 kms

- 🕐 Allow 5 hours to include visits to museums

- ▭ Pavements, lanes and roads

- P Car parks in High Street and Kirkstyle

- T There is a bus service from Lanark, which is served by trains to Glasgow

- 🍴 Various cafés, restaurants, hotels, pubs and shops in Biggar

- WC Biggar Kirk Gillespie Centre

- I Tourist Information Centre open Easter to October, Tel. (01899) 21066. Albion Motors Archive, Tel. (01899) 21050

medieval layout, with a broad High Street designed to house a market. Most of the prominent buildings are Victorian, though a few date from the 17th and 18th centuries.

The walk begins at perhaps the oldest structure in the town, Cadger's Brig **Ⓐ**, a bridge over Biggar Burn. Legend has it that in 1297 William Wallace crossed it disguised as a cadger, or pedlar, to spy on Edward I's army.

The bridge is on the way to the Gas Works **Ⓑ**. The building, which dates from 1839, houses a small museum of early gas appliances, and the production of coal gas is explained by a video show.

MOAT PARK

It is just a short step to Burn Braes **Ⓒ**, a grassy valley through which gurgles the little Biggar Burn. It incorporates Moat Park, with a play area that includes an exciting aerial ropeway. At one end of Burn Braes

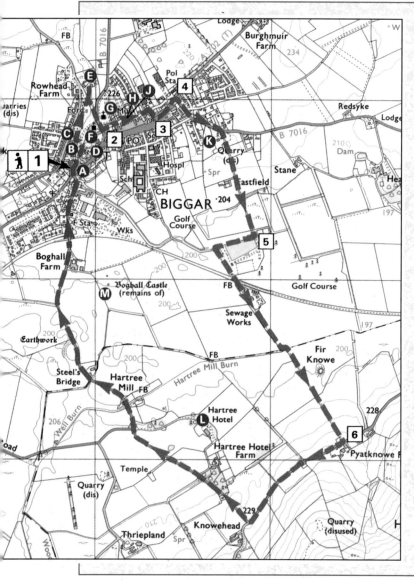

BIGGAR – HARTREE – BOGHALL CASTLE

The walk starts at Cadger's Brig Ⓐ behind the war memorial in Biggar.

▶1 Walk up Gas Works Road to the Gas Works Ⓑ and museum. At the end of the road, take the path through Burn Braes Ⓒ, passing Motte Knowe Ⓓ on your right. At a road called Kirkstyle, turn left to leave an aerial ropeway on your left. Fork left down a steep, narrow road over a shallow ford to Biggar Mill car park, then cross a footbridge over the burn to Greenhill Farmhouse Ⓔ. Return to Kirkstyle and continue along it past Moat Park Heritage Centre Ⓕ on your right, then Old Kirk Ⓖ on your left.

▶2 Turn left into North Back Road to Gladstone Court Museum Ⓗ and the Albion Motors Archive Ⓙ on your left. Turn right into Lambie's Close to reach the High Street.

▶3 Turn left and continue walking for 300 yards (275m) to a crossroads by the police station.

▶4 Turn right along a road signposted to Broughton. Take the third turning to the right to head down Park Road, signposted for the Puppet Theatre Ⓚ (on the right) and the Golf Club ahead.

▶5 At the golf shop, turn right beside a boating pond, then left. Continue past a caravan park, over a footbridge, across dismantled railway lines, and straight on past the sewage works on your left. Beyond Fir Knowe, a small drumlin left by an Ice Age glacier, you reach a road by Pyatknowe Farm.

▶6 Turn right. After ½ mile (800m), you come to a T-junction. Turn right up the lane (signposted to Biggar), and continue past Hartree Hotel Ⓛ and then the remains of Boghall Castle Ⓜ away to your right. The lane becomes Station Road, and ends opposite Cadger's Brig.

is Motte Knowe Ⓓ, a rounded hump that was the site of a Norman motte and bailey castle. At the other end is Greenhill Farmhouse Ⓔ, which now houses a museum, the subject of which is the Covenanters, the Presbyterians persecuted by the Crown in the 17th century.

HERITAGE CENTRE

Between the two is Moat Park Heritage Centre Ⓕ, which contains a fascinating and clearly-presented history of the region. Its models of crannogs, brochs and other ancient buildings are as good as, if not better than, those in more famous museums. Spitting Image has donated an image of the 18th-century

◀ *Biggar's old Gas Works, now open to visitors, has an interesting museum illustrating how gas was produced.*

JOHN WATNEY

◀Housed in the old works building is the Albion Motors Archive, where records and photographs have been kept of the company's fine old vehicles. In the Moat Park Heritage Centre, set up by the Biggar Museum Trust, this model of an ancient broch (below) is one of many exhibits that bring the history of the area to life.

political cartoonist, James Gillray, whose father was a local blacksmith.

On the opposite side of the road stands the Old Kirk **G**. The large 'throuch-stane', or tombstone, in the churchyard is marked with 150 years of Gladstone family names, ending with Thomas W Gladstone (died 1856), a cousin of the famous 19th-century Whig Prime Minister.

Just along North Back Road is the Gladstone Court Museum **H**, dedicated to the great man. This unusual memorial takes the form of a miniature street of Biggar shops and offices — a bank, a chemist, a shoe-maker's, a dressmaker's and other tradesmen — reconstructed and stocked as they were in his day.

Perhaps the most fascinating exhibit in the museum is a 1900 Albion motor car, worth £40,000, which the Museum Trust bought in Honolulu. The car began its life in the Albion Motor Works, just behind Gladstone Court. The company was started in 1899 by Thomas Black-wood Murray with a capital of £1,300 raised by mortgaging the family farm. He is believed to have built the first British car made entirely by one man.

MOTORS ARCHIVE

Albion later became the largest lorry-building firm in the British Empire, and is today once more an independent firm. Part of the old works is now the repository of the Albion Motors Archive **J** with many thousands of photographs which may be inspected by prior arrangement.

The route makes its way out of the town past its most entertaining attraction, the International Purves Puppet Theatre **K**. A scaled-up version of the Victorian 'penny plain,

◀The stone-built Greenhill Farmhouse now contains a museum detailing the history of the Covenanters.

tuppence coloured' toy theatres, it boasts high-tech sound and lighting, and seating for over 100 people.

The puppets are illuminated by ultra-violet spotlights, and their bright costumes and painted fea-tures fluoresce on the darkened stage. There are matinees during most of the year, but seats must be booked in advance. Between shows, visitors are shown round a museum of antique puppets and taken back-stage to meet the 'cast' and their puppet-masters.

Once you are out of the town, the walk heads through farmland where Aberdeen Angus cattle and

Clydesdale horses are bred. Further on, the lower slopes of the Hartree Hills give views back over the placid Upper Clyde Valley to Biggar and the hills beyond.

You return to Biggar along a quiet road. A short diversion up a drive leads to Hartree House ⓛ, a Grade II listed building in the Victorian Scottish Baronial style; parts of the house date back to the 15th century. It is now a country-house hotel, but non-residents are welcome to pass over the marble-paved threshold to admire the interior, whether or not they take a drink or a meal. The dining-room ceiling is a copy of that in Mary, Queen of Scots' bedroom in the Palace of Holyroodhouse in Edinburgh.

▶ *Where the route passes Pyatknowe Farm, there is a fine view over watermeadows to Broughton Heights.*

JOHN WATNEY

Working with Gas

In the 1780s, the 9th Duke of Dundonald was heating coal to make tar when he realized that it was giving off an inflammable gas. He collected some of the gas in a retort and used it to fuel lights around his home. The first man to use gas commercially in Britain was also a Scot, William Murdoch (1754-1839). He installed a gas lighting system for the firm of Boulton and Watt, of James Watt fame, in Birmingham in 1798.

At first, gas works were custom-built for every private house or workshop using the fuel. The first supply piped to the public was installed in London in 1812 by the chartered Gas Light and Coke Company, formed by German-born Friedrich Winzer.

The Biggar Gas Works, opened in 1839, was among the pioneer suppliers of gas to small towns. Coal gas, or town gas as it was often called, was made by baking coal in sealed retorts of cast iron. The result had to be purified and scrubbed before it could be used, and the whole process produced useful by-products. Coke went to market-garden greenhouses, to large homes for central heating and to bakers to heat their ovens. Tar went to the Scottish Tar Distilleries, and ammonia to bleach makers. Whenever the purifiers were cleaned, local children with whooping cough were taken to the works to inhale the sulphur fumes, which were thought to have medicinal qualities. Gas manufacture ceased in Biggar on 4 January 1973.

NATIONAL MUSEUMS OF SCOTLAND

This contemporary lithograph shows the Biggar Gas Works and the surrounding village houses as they were in 1873, 100 years before production ceased.

▼*Built in the Scottish Baronial style, 1 mile (1.6km) to the south of Biggar, Hartree House is now a grand hotel.*

JOHN WATNEY

This country section of the walk twice crosses the border from Clydesdale into Tweeddale. Going from one to the other, the colour of the road changes from ochre to black. Soon after the second of these changes, and just before the boundaries of the town, is Boghall Farm. Behind the farmhouse, in a field, are the scant remains of medieval Boghall Castle ⓜ, the former home of Lord Fleming.

BURNS' HOMELAND

A riverside walk in the heart of Burns country

Although Alloway is now a suburb of Ayr, it has a long history as a separate village in its own right as well as many associations with its most famous son, Robert Burns. The poet was born in 1759 in a 'clay biggin', which has been preserved as one of the best surviving examples of traditional rural housing in the western Lowlands.

THE FAMILY HOME

The cottage **Ⓐ** is single-storey and thatched, with walls of solid clay. It is protected from the weather by harling (a kind of roughcast) and whitewash and was designed to accommodate people at one end and livestock at the other. The living end is divided into two sections, the 'but' and the 'ben'. The former is the kitchen and communal living area and the latter the private sleeping

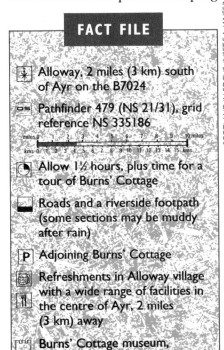

SCOTLAND IN FOCUS. INSET:E.A. JANES/NHPA

▲In Burns' poem, Tam O'Shanter escaped from witches across Alloway's 13th-century Old Bridge of Doon. Honey fungus (left) grows on damp wood such as this fallen beech tree.

18th-century tombstones. Burns' father William (who used the old spelling of their surname – Burness) is buried here. The building, which was ruined in Burns' day, is best known for its association with one of his most famous poems, *Tam O'Shanter*. Riding home from Ayr in the midst of a storm, the

FACT FILE

✈ Alloway, 2 miles (3 km) south of Ayr on the B7024

▭ Pathfinder 479 (NS 21/31), grid reference NS 335186

miles 0 1 2 3 4 5 6 7 8 9 10 miles
kms 0 1 2 3 4 5 6 7 8 9 10 11 12 13 14 15 kms

🕐 Allow 1½ hours, plus time for a tour of Burns' Cottage

▭ Roads and a riverside footpath (some sections may be muddy after rain)

P Adjoining Burns' Cottage

🍴 Refreshments in Alloway village with a wide range of facilities in the centre of Ayr, 2 miles (3 km) away

🏛 Burns' Cottage museum, open all year. Land O'Burns Centre, open all year. Burns' Monument, open all year

room, which would have been for the head of the family and his wife. The cottage contains period furniture, some of which belonged to the Burns family, and was supposedly built by the poet's father. Although it may seem crude by modern standards, it was quite a substantial and well-built dwelling in its day. Next door there is a small museum which contains an extensive collection of Burns' manuscripts and letters.

TAM O'SHANTER

Overlooking the valley of the River Doon stands the roofless shell of Alloway's historic old parish kirk **Ⓑ**, surrounded by a fine collection of

SCOTLAND IN FOCUS

▼The cottage where the poet Robert Burns grew up was built by his father, who was an Ayrshire farmer.

THE WALK

ALLOWAY

The walk begins outside Burns' Cottage Ⓐ in the centre of Alloway.

1 Follow the B7024 southwards to Alloway Kirk Ⓑ. Almost opposite the church, a side road leads to the Land O' Burns Centre Ⓒ. After visiting the centre, return to the main road.

2 Carry on towards the River Doon, but before reaching the river take a side road to the left to the Burns Monument Ⓓ.

3 Carry on past the monument and cross the river by the Old Bridge of Doon Ⓔ. Continue uphill until you rejoin the B7024. Turn right and recross the river by the New Bridge until you are back at Alloway Kirk.

4 A short distance beyond the church, turn left down a side road that leads to the river and continue along the riverside path. Climb uphill past the driveway to Cambusdoon House Ⓕ.

5 Follow the road through a housing estate to a T-junction. Turn right and follow the road back to the B7024 and Burns' Cottage where the walk began.

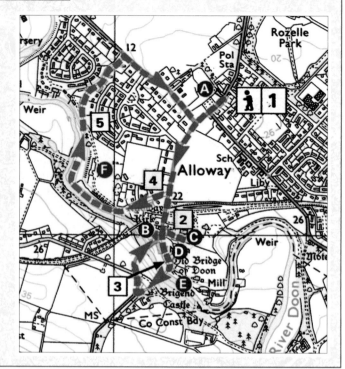

drunken Tam stumbled upon a gathering of witches among the ruins of the old church. He watched their revels until, taken by the dancing of a beautiful young witch, Nannie, he shouted out to encourage her and then had to gallop for his life with the witches in hot pursuit.

LIFE-SIZE STATUES

The Land O'Burns Centre Ⓒ, which is open all year, contains a theatre where you can see a multi-screen presentation about the life and times of the poet as well as an exhibition concerning the places that are associated with him. Closer to the river is a monument Ⓓ to the poet, erected in 1823. The garden in which it stands contains full-size statues of the incautious Tam and his drinking crony Souter Johnnie.

The River Doon is spanned by the Old Bridge Ⓔ, a high-arched struc-

▼*The walk passes through the beautifully maintained gardens that surround the ruins of Cambusdoon.*

ture reputed to date from the 13th century. Today it is restricted to pedestrian traffic. In Burns' poem, when Tam was fleeing from the witches on Meg, his grey mare, he escaped by crossing the bridge over the river. His pursuers could not follow him across running water but Nannie, fleet of foot, was right on his heels and as Meg reached the keystone she grasped the horse's tail and pulled it off!

From the crest of the bridge there is a fine view of the famous 'banks and braes of bonnie Doon' that were immortalized by the poet. The woods on the far side of the river form part of the Doon estate where Robert's father once worked as a gardener. A short distance upstream are the remains of Brigend Castle.

CAMBUSDOON

From the New Bridge there is a good view of the steep-sided valley through which the River Doon runs its course. Further downstream and above the path are the ruins of Cambusdoon House Ⓕ. The house was constructed for a local industrialist. When it was built in the early 19th-century, it was an imposing mansion in the Scottish Baronial style. The surrounding gardens and woods are still well maintained.

A walk around a small monastic town on the River Tyne

The attractive market town of Hexham, set in the beautiful Tynedale valley, is dominated by its fine abbey, which dates from Saxon times. Like many of England's border towns, it once suffered at the hands of the Scots, but now it is a peaceful, bustling place, popular with tourists visiting nearby Hadrian's Wall. There are several interesting historical buildings, a weekly market, and plenty of green, open spaces, as well as lovely walks in the surrounding countryside.

MANOR OFFICE

This walk, though, concentrates on the town itself. Near the start is the Manor Office **Ⓐ**, built as a prison in 1330-32 by the Archbishop of York. It was the first building in England to be specially built for this purpose, and was used as such until 1824. Today, it houses a captivating Border History Museum, and the Tourist Information Centre.

A little further on is the Moot

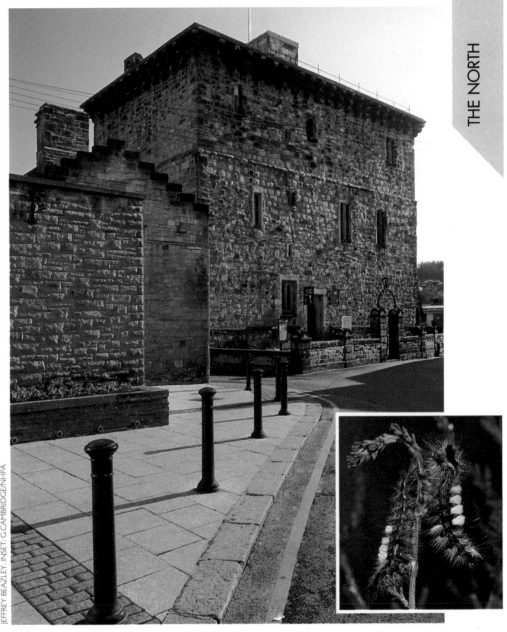

JEFFREY BEAZLEY. INSET: G.CAMBRIDGE/NHPA

▲ *The 14th-century Manor Office, near the start of the walk, was the first purpose-built prison in England. The caterpillar (inset) of the widespread vapourer moth is highly distinctive.*

FACT FILE

- ☀ Hexham, 20 miles (32km) west of Newcastle, off the A69

- ⊙ˢ Pathfinder 547 (NY 86/96), grid reference NY 938641

  miles 0 1 2 3 4 5 6 7 8 9 10 miles
  kms 0 1 2 3 4 5 6 7 8 9 10 11 12 13 14 15 kms

- 🕐 1 hour

- ▭ Pavements and good paths

- Ⓣ Regular coach and train services to and from Newcastle and Carlisle

- Ⓟ Car park at start

- 🍴 Numerous pubs, restaurants and cafés in the town

- wc By car park at start

- Ⓘ Tourist Information Centre at Manor Office

Hall **Ⓑ**, which dates from the 14th century, and was once the residence of the Archbishops of York. This impressive tower house is the only defensive structure in Hexham. Its walls are 11 feet (3.3m) thick in places. An archway leads through to the Market Place and a long shelter known as the Shambles, where colourful stalls are set out every Tuesday. Hexham is the centre of a large agricultural community, and there is also a weekly livestock market, one of the busiest in the country.

On the other side of Market Place is Hexham's abbey **Ⓒ**, founded in AD674 when Queen Ethelreda of Northumbria gave land to her spiritual adviser, Wilfrid. The abbey is set in lovely grounds with well-kept lawns. The original building incorporated stones from the Roman fort of Corstopitum. Much of the present abbey, dedicated to St Andrew, dates

THE WALK

HEXHAM

The walk begins at the large car park by Wentworth Leisure Centre and Safeway.

➡ Walk up the path beside Wentworth Café, and follow a sign to the Tourist Information Centre in Manor Office **A**. Continue to Moot Hall **B**. An archway leads through to Market Place, and Hexham Abbey **C** is clearly visible on the other side.

➡ After visiting the abbey, turn right out of the entrance along Beaumont Street. Turn right through the memorial arch gateway into the Abbey Grounds.

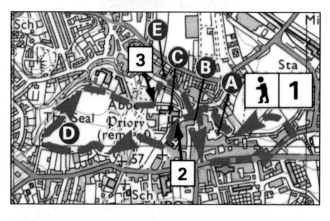

Follow a footpath towards the bandstand. Over a stream, bear left and follow a path uphill through beech trees to a gateway in the corner. Go through the gateway, and follow the path uphill, with cottages on your left and the Seal **D** on your right. At the end of a stone wall, turn right along the far side of the Seal. This path bears right, and descends steps to a metalled path heading back towards the abbey, past a school on the left and a playground area on the right. Keep ahead down Cowgarth.

➡ Just before an archway leading to the abbey on your right, turn left towards the Priory Gatehouse **E**. Turn right along Market Street to Market Place. Cross to the Moot Hall side, and go down Fore Street to the Midland Bank. Turn left along Priestpopple. Bear left at a mini-roundabout, then turn left into a side street back to the car park where the walk began.

BOTH PHOTOS: JEFFREY BEAZLEY

from the 12th century, but there is also a superb Saxon bishops' chair — in which the Saxon Kings of Northumbria were crowned — cut from a solid block of sandstone.

ABBEY GROUNDS

The walk continues up Beaumont Street towards the Queens Hall, built in 1865-66 in a French château-style. It is now a multi-purpose Arts Centre, with a theatre and a library. A gateway opposite the Queens Hall, a memorial arch to those who died in World War I, leads into the Abbey Grounds. You follow a footpath past a war memorial to reach a jolly Edwardian bandstand. There

▲ *The Moot Hall, a 14th-century tower house, now houses a library. Hexham Abbey (below right) overlooks delightful grounds with a bandstand.*

are lovely glimpses of the abbey through the trees, particularly in the spring and autumn.

The path crosses a small burn and continues right round the Seal or Sele **D**, a large, gently sloping hill on the western side of the Abbey Grounds. This lovely open space, once a place of meditation for monks, is now a public park.

On the other side of the Seal, you pass through the Priory Gatehouse **E** (St Wilfrid's Gateway) on the site of the original AD674-680 cathedral, which was destroyed by the Danes in AD821. The Gatehouse dates from the time of the Augustinian Canons, who built a priory in 1114-40. There was an almonry here, where the Hexham monks cared for pilgrims and the poor.

Beyond the gateway is Market Street, the old main street of Hexham, which has interesting shops and buildings. This leads back to the Market Place, where the pedestrianized Fore Street takes you to an unusual, late Victorian triangular building, with a wealth of architectural detail, which now houses the Midland Bank. At the junction, you go left down Priestpopple – which, together with Battle Hill to the right, makes up the main street through the modern town – to return to the start.

OLD NEWCASTLE

JEFFREY BEAZLEY

A stroll around the medieval heart of a modern city

Newcastle is a vibrant city whose origins date back to Roman times. Its name comes from the 'new castle' built by the son of William the Conqueror in 1080. The city today still has one of the finest Norman keeps in the country, as well as medieval houses, superb Victorian architecture, modern shopping centres, an excellent Metro rapid transport system, and theatres and art galleries. A major industrial centre, it prospered in the 18th and 19th centuries from the coal trade.

GREY'S MONUMENT

The walk starts at Grey's Monument **A**, in the heart of the city, built to mark the passing of the Great Reform Bill of 1832. The 135-foot (50-m) column is open on Saturdays and Bank Holidays, and those prepared to climb its steps are rewarded with a superb view over

PAUL STEVENS/SWIFT PICTURE LIBRARY

▲*Favourite resting places for the urban-dwelling starling are ledges, telephone wires and overhead power lines.*

the city. From the Monument, Blackett Street leads between the splendid Art Nouveau Emerson Chambers, with its richly detailed facade, and the modernistic Eldon Square Shopping Centre.

The route joins the top of Newgate Street. Opposite you is St Andrew's Church **B**, the city's oldest church, with parts dating from the 12th century. The elaborate

▲*Reflected in the exterior of a modern building is the richly ornamented, Art Nouveau facade of Emerson Chambers.*

FACT FILE

✳ Newcastle-upon-Tyne

OS Pathfinder 549 (NZ 26/36), grid reference NZ 248644

miles 0 1 2 3 4 5 6 7 8 9 10 miles
kms 0 1 2 3 4 5 6 7 8 9 10 11 12 13 14 15 kms

◗ Allow at least 1½ hours

▬ Town walk on pavements; some steep steps

P Various signposted car parks close to city centre; meter parking in streets

T Well served by coaches, buses, trains and Metro

🍴 Numerous pubs, restaurants, cafés and toilets in the city

I Tourist information at the Central Library in Princess Square and at Central Station concourse, Tel. (0191) 261 0691

THE WALK

NEWCASTLE

The walk begins at Grey's Monument **A**, *at the top of Grey Street, which can be reached by taking the Metro to Monument Station.*

1 Leave the square by Blackett Street, past Dillons bookshop, to Newgate Street. Turn left. St Andrew's Church **B** is on the other side of the road. Past the church take the street on the right (St Andrew's Street) and follow it to a public house (Rosie's Bar) at the top, on the corner of Stowell Street. Just beyond the pub, turn left down a narrow alley (West Walls), and follow it to the far end at Heber Tower. Then turn left, cross Stowell Street and walk down Friars Street to Blackfriars **C**.

2 Walk back up Friars Street to Stowell Street. Turn left, then left again and walk down beside the town walls in Bath Lane. Turn left into Westgate Road, then take the first left into Cross Street, adjoining Charlotte Square. Turn right into Fenkle Street. Follow this to where it joins Westgate

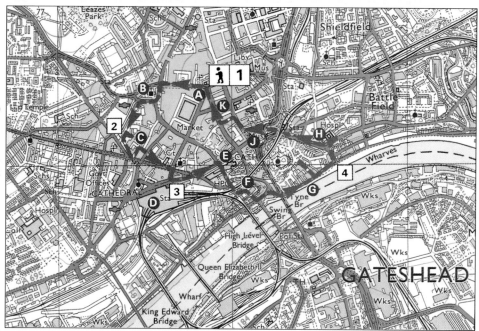

Road by the Assembly Rooms. Turn left to walk down Westgate Road, then right at the junction with Grainger Street to Central Station **D**.

3 Turn left down Neville Street towards the Stephenson Monument, then go straight on down Collingwood Street to St Nicholas's Cathedral **E**. Turn right down St Nicholas Street, go past the Black Gate and under the railway bridge, then turn left to the entrance to The Keep **F**. After visiting The Keep, cross Castle Garth

and descend Castle Stairs to the Quayside **G**. Follow the Quayside, past the Swing Bridge and the Guildhall. Go under the Tyne Bridge and after passing King Street, turn left into Broad Chare to visit the Trinity Maritime Centre and Trinity House. Return to the Quayside and then continue past the Law Courts.

4 At the end of the Quayside, bear left, cross the road and go up past the Barley Mow Pub, with the Keelman's Hospital **H** opposite. Cross the road

here and turn left into City Road and follow this to the Corner Tower. Go under the railway bridge, cross the road via a subway and bear right in the subway to reach the Joicey Museum **J**. From the museum, return to the subway, continuing straight on and then turning right to reach the Royal Arcade. Signs indicate the way to Pilgrim Street. Turn right up Pilgrim Street and take the next left (High Bridge). Turn right up Grey Street, passing the Theatre Royal **K**, to Grey's Monument.

15th-century font cover is one of the finest in England. Some of the town walls are visible in the churchyard.

Further on, a narrow alley known as West Walls, just off St Andrew's Street, has the longest remaining stretch of Newcastle's 13th-century town walls. John Leland, a 16th-century historian, stated that Newcastle was one of the finest walled towns of Europe. Originally, the walls were about 2 miles (3.2km) in length and up to 25 feet (7.5m) in height. At the end of this section is Heber Tower,

◀ *Blackfriars, a substantial 13th-century Dominican abbey, now houses a restaurant and craft workshops.*

the best preserved of all the medieval wall towers.

Signs point the way to Blackfriars **C**, founded by the Dominicans in the 13th century, and now restored with a restaurant and various craft workshops around the old cloister. Just beyond, in Bath Lane, there is an uninterrupted view of a substantial section of the town walls.

18TH-CENTURY SQUARE

From the bottom of Bath Lane, the route continues along Westgate Road and into Cross Street, leading to Charlotte Square, Newcastle's only formal 18th-century square. Between here and the Assembly

JEFFREY BEAZLEY

ALL PHOTOS JEFFREY BEAZLEY

Continue down Collingwood Street to St Nicholas's Cathedral **E**. This was originally a parish church, raised to cathedral status in 1882. Its chief architectural glory is the lantern tower with its crown spire of about 1470, rising to a height of 193 feet (58m). There is a tradition that in 1644, during the siege of Newcastle, the Scottish army threatened to blow up the church with cannon fire, but the mayor put his Scottish prisoners in the lantern tower and thus saved it from destruction.

SQUARE NORMAN KEEP

From here you head towards the river, following St Nicholas Street to the Black Gate, the entrance to the massive castle Keep **F**. The original 'new castle' of 1080 was built of wood; Henry II started on the stone building visible today in 1168. It is one of Britain's finest examples of a square Norman Keep. The roof commands an excellent view of Newcastle and Gateshead, and of the River Tyne running between.

Castle Stairs descend steeply to the Quayside **G**, with good views of some of the six Tyne bridges nearby. The High Level Bridge on the right, built by Robert Stephenson in 1846-49, was a great engineering achievement for its time. The Swing Bridge, almost immediately ahead, was built in 1876 on the site of Newcastle's Roman, medieval and 18th-century bridges. Pons Aelius, the name by which Newcastle was known in Roman times, means 'the settlement with a bridge'.

This area was the historical core of Newcastle until the building of the High Level Bridge, which took away the main traffic into and out of

Rooms was the most fashionable area of late Georgian Newcastle.

St John's Church, at the junction with Grainger Street, dates mostly from the 14th and 15th centuries. Along with St Andrew's, it is one of the four original parish churches of Newcastle. Close by, Central Station **D** is one of the greatest monuments to the English railway age, and was opened by Queen Victoria in 1850. A large traffic island contains a monument to the memory of George Stephenson, the prime mover behind the world's first steam railway, the Stockton–Darlington line. He was born and raised locally.

▶*The elegant 17th-century Guildhall is one of many fine buildings in Quayside, which, since 1928, has nestled under the impressive Tyne Bridge (below). Another showpiece is St Nicholas's Cathedral (above left), which its magnificent lantern tower, seen here from The Keep.*

the city. With the decrease of the city's maritime interests and the new commercial developments of Richard Grainger, the importance of the Quayside steadily declined until recent efforts to revitalize the area began. There are some fine buildings here, such as the 17th-century Guildhall, with its magnificent Merchant Adventurers' Court and Great Hall, and some tall, timber-framed merchants' houses.

TYNE BRIDGE

Passing under the 1928 Tyne Bridge, similar in shape, if not size, to the Sydney Harbour Bridge, there is a good view up King Street to All Saints, one of the finest Georgian churches in the country. In Broad Chare, beyond the Baltic Tavern, is

the Trinity Maritime Centre, a museum devoted to shipping and the River Tyne. Next door is Trinity House, with its beautiful courtyard. Returning to the Quayside, the route passes the impressive new building housing the Law Courts, then bears left towards the Keelman's Hospital ⓗ, built in 1701 to provide accommodation for poor, aged or disabled keelmen and their widows. The keels were the flat-bottomed lighters that brought coal from the pits upstream to the colliers in the port. Nearby is the Sallyport Tower and then, further along City Road, the Corner Tower, another fragment of the town wall, with excellent views of All Saints Church.

JOICEY MUSEUM

The route turns back towards the city centre, passing the Holy Jesus Hospital of 1681, a fine example of old brickwork, which now houses the Joicey Museum of Newcastle's social history ⓙ. A subway leads to Pilgrim Street where a left turn leads to the magnificent Grey Street. In the 1830s, this area of central Newcastle was extensively developed in the classical style by Richard Grainger, who successfully completed old Eldon Square, the New Markets,

▲*Central Arcade, built in 1906, echoes the classical style of the Theatre Royal (right), with its splendid columned portico, which was constructed in the 1830s by Richard Grainger.*

several major streets and the Theatre Royal. Grainger worked closely with the architect John Dobson, who also designed Central Station.

Grey Street stretches down towards the river from Grey's Monument. Wide and generously proportioned, it is often cited as one of the most graceful streets in Europe. The Theatre Royal ⓚ, with its impressive portico of giant

columns, is the third home of the Royal Shakespeare Company and was extensively refurbished in 1987-8. Perhaps the finest of the other notable buildings in the street is the present Lloyds Bank at the corner of Hood Street.

Between Grey Street, Market Street and Grainger Street are the Exchange Buildings, also built by Grainger. The interior was badly damaged by fire, and in 1906 was replaced by the Central Arcade, with its iron and glass roof, and tiled floor with classical motifs. A short stroll takes you back to the start.

Cunard's transatlantic passenger liner Mauretania *made her maiden voyage from the Tyne in November 1907.*

were built. Newcastle's Quayside was the centre of Tyneside's maritime trade, and in its heyday, during the 19th century, was one of the busiest and most prosperous commercial areas in England.

By the beginning of the 20th century, many Tyneside companies had merged to build huge ocean-going ships such as the liner *Mauretania*, powered by steam turbines that generated 70,000 horse-power (52.2MW) and allowed an average cruising speed of 24 knots (44.5kmh). Until 1913, Tyneside led the world in the building of oil tankers. The World Wars saw the shipyards busy with naval contracts, but ever since there has been a decline. Today, some employment is provided by oil rigs brought to the yards for repairs.

Tyneside Shipyards

Ships have been built on the River Tyne since the Middle Ages, most of them associated with the coal trade. Keels, or lighters, carried the coal from the mines and staithes higher up the river to the sea-going colliers. The Tyne keels were flat-bottomed, oval boats with square sails and two long oars. The colliers were made of Baltic timber, with

sails of Baltic flax, and were built in many of the small shipyards along both sides of the Tyne.

Some of the first iron ships were launched here in the 1840s. In 1852, a screw-driven collier was built, capable of carrying 650 tons of coal to London within 48 hours. At this time, the river was dredged to give a deeper channel, and new quays, docks, jetties and piers

THE PROUD TOWERS

9

THE NORTH

AA PICTURE LIBRARY. INSET. J & M BAIN/NHPA

A northern cathedral city on the banks of the River Wear

It is a strange anomaly that, in a country which is flattest to the east, England's three most visually dominant cathedrals — Ely, Lincoln, and Durham **D** — stand proudly raised against eastern skies. To appreciate the cathedral fully it is necessary to view the city initially from a distance, and on foot.

This walk avoids any parking and traffic problems in Durham, and threads its way along the lightly wooded banks of the River Wear into the very heart of the city.

ST CUTHBERT

From the river bank under Pelaw Wood **A** a grand, complete outline of Durham Cathedral comes into view. Further along the route its twin pinnacled towers can be seen to the right; they are balanced beau-

---

FACT FILE

* Durham, County Durham

* Pathfinder 572 (NZ 24/34), grid reference NZ 287410

miles 0 1 2 3 4 5 6 7 8 9 10 miles
kms 0 1 2 3 4 5 6 7 8 9 10 11 12 13 14 15 kms

* 5 hours, including visits to cathedral and castle

* A gentle climb to the cathedral. Riverside paths can be muddy

* **P** Adjacent to Shincliffe Bridge in a lane signposted 'Houghall Farm and Gardens'

* Rose Tree Inn across Shincliffe Bridge. Cathedral coffee shop and toilets

---

tifully on the left by smaller turrets. Nearby is Durham Castle, sharing this near-island site.

Durham has several bridges. New Elvet Bridge **B** was built in the 12th century as a second river cross-

---

▲*Durham Cathedral, on the River Wear, was begun in 1093 and completed 40 years later. Common comfrey (inset) has been used in medicines for centuries and can be eaten when cooked.*

ing. Of its 14 arches only 12 are now visible, while its chapel and medieval houses have disappeared. The cathedral was built as a shrine for the body of St Cuthbert, replacing an earlier Saxon Church on this site. St Cuthbert died in 687AD, but apparently, 11 years later his body was found to be undecayed.

DANISH RAIDS

To escape Danish raids in the 9th century, the monks who were caring for his remains began travelling throughout the north, taking the body of the saint with them. It was over 100 years before they built a church in Durham. Enshrined over a century later, St Cuthbert's body was still well preserved and the fame of this and his great holiness brought vast numbers of pilgrims

THE WALK

DURHAM

The walk begins next to Shincliffe Bridge in a lane signposted 'Hougall Farm and Gardens'.

1 Cross the road, heading for the river bank. You will see a thread of red hilltop houses ahead. A good path leads to a foot suspension bridge, cross it and continue straight across a playing field to reach another footbridge over a stream. Continue straight on between the red brick cheeks of a derelict railway arch. The path turns left to follow a wooded stream back to the River Wear, which is quite a sizeable river here. There is a better path ahead, following along under Pelaw Wood **A** towards the city.

2 The riverside path continues, flanking the newish buildings of England's third oldest university. Ignore the first two bridges, but at the third take flight of steps up to old Elvet Bridge **B**.

3 Turn right into an attractive stone-clad thoroughfare rising towards Saddler Street and the market place **C**. Now turn left along Silver Street, to cross the River Wear once again at Framwellgate.

4 Go left round two sides of 'The Fighting Cocks', taking the part-cobbled South Street which rises steadily to afford splendid views of the cathedral. Beyond the top of the hill at the junction with South Street turn left through a gap in the stone wall, which gives access to a path through woodland, down to Prebends Bridge.

5 Cross the bridge, then take the upper of the two paths on the left, rising towards the cathedral **D**. At the top, keep to the left-hand path which passes under the west end of the cathedral. Turn right at top of next rise between high walling and come out onto Palace Green. The north door of the cathedral with its sanctuary knocker is on the right. Enter the cathedral.

6 Leave the cathedral Treasury, return through the cloisters and exit at the south-east corner into the College. Turn left through archway at the east turning left into North Bailey. Pass east end of the cathedral and turn right to Palace Green. Ahead is Durham Castle **E**, part of the university and open to the public (restricted during term time).

7 Leave the castle and walk into Saddler Street which leads down to Elvet Bridge. From Stage 3 retrace your steps to the start of the walk.

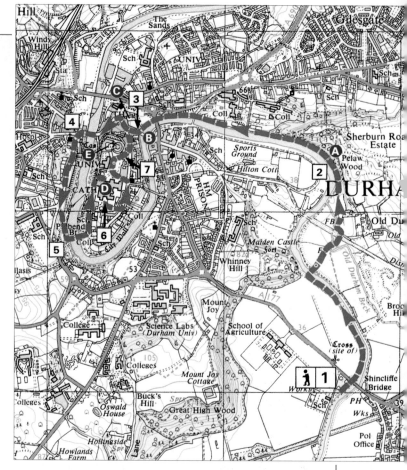

▲ *Framwellgate Bridge, partly constructed of York stone, has been a pedestrian bridge since 1975.*

▶ *Prior Castell's clock survived after 3,000 Scots were kept prisoner in the cathedral after the Battle of Dunbar.*

and enormous wealth to his shrine. St Cuthbert's earliest coffin, his pectoral cross and unique embroidered stoles are now on display in the Cathedral Treasury.

LAY RULERS

Durham Castle **E** occupies the second most commanding position in the city. The Crypt Chapel is probably all that remains of the castle built in 1072, while the keep dates from 1840. Between the two is ranged a curve of buildings spanning the centuries when the bishops of Durham were lay rulers as well as religious leaders.

MIKE WILLIAMS. INSET: BOB CHAPMAN/NATURE PHOTOGRAPHERS LTD

way along the hills, is 18½ miles (30 km) long. It runs along the gritstone escarpment from Lyme Hall in the north to Rushton in the south.

The Macclesfield Canal **D** was fully operational in 1831 and is 27³/₄ miles (45 km) long with 13

◀ *The town of Bollington, on the edge of the Pennines, seen from the vantage point of White Nancy. Growing by local canals, flowering rush (inset) blooms from July to August in wet habitats.*

FACT FILE

* ✳ 3 miles (4.8 km) north-east of Macclesfield

* ⊡ Pathfinder 759 (SJ 87/97), grid reference SJ 931781

miles 0 1 2 3 4 5 6 7 8 9 10 miles
kms 0 1 2 3 4 5 6 7 8 9 10 11 12 13 14 15 kms

* ◔ Allow 2 hours

* ▭ Steep hill climb at beginning then gradual descent, followed by level canal walking. Mainly well defined paths, some road walking; walking boots advised

* P North-western edge of Bollington, close to the Middlewood Way and Macclesfield Canal; just off the B5090 road

* ▦ Numerous inns passed on walk — Vale Inn, Queens Arms, and Red Lion Inn in Bollington. On the canal the Barge Inn

* WC In car park

* **I** Information centre at Adelphi Mill. Information and Ranger centre at car park

A bracing walk to a vantage point over the Cheshire Plain

The route is on field paths and along towpaths and after the initial steep ascent is mostly level walking. White Nancy **B** and the Saddle of Kerridge is an exceptional vantage point with extensive views over the Cheshire Plain. Being the end of the Pennines the hills make a dramatic rise from the plain. Along these hills you follow a section of the Gritstone Trail **C** before descending to the canal, passing mills, aqueducts and narrowboats.

The town of Bollington **A** is dominated by the 1,000-foot (305-metre) high ridge of Kerridge. There were numerous mills here that were driven by power from the many streams and later by coal carried on the canal. The last cotton mill ceased operating in 1960. Many of the mills and houses are built from stone quarried from Kerridge Hill.

The prominent and renowned landmark of White Nancy is a cylindrical white painted dome. It is believed to have been built by the Gaskell family to commemorate the Battle of Waterloo. Nancy was a member of the family.

The full route of the Gritstone Trail, which you follow for a short

THE WALK

BOLLINGTON – MACCLESFIELD CANAL

The walk begins in Bollington **A**, *from Adlington Road car park beside the Middlewood Way. Most of it is walked in a clockwise direction.*

1 Walk out of the car park and turn right along Adlington Road to main road junction and turn left along Palmerston Street. Walk under the Bollington Aqueduct and turn right along Water Street to its junction with High Street beside the Queens Arms. Turn right along High Street ascending to the Red Lion Inn. Turn left and at the end of the row of houses (at the start of Cow Lane) is the path sign and stile for White Nancy and Saddle of Kerridge.

2 Turn right and ascend steeply, close to the field boundary on your right, to a stile. Go through this and take a flight of stone steps to the next stile, just ahead through the wall on the left and continue your ascent. Cross a track and continue ascending to the white-topped monument — White Nancy **B**. (This is steep and can be slippery in wet weather so footwear should have a good grip.)

3 Walk along the crest of the Saddle of Kerridge (part of the Gritstone Trail **C**) with the wall on your left to a stile. Continue, after 27 yards (25 metres) cross wall using obvious stile. After this keep the wall on your right along the crest to the next stile. Then keep wall on left and continue until three field walls converge at a stile. Don't cross the stile, but turn right at the 'Danger – Fenced Quarry Face' sign. Descend the path by the wall to a stile and continue descending with an old (Endon) quarry on your right, down to the old quarry track. Turn left to a minor road.

4 Cross over minor road and take footpath signposted to your right and walk down the track towards Endon Hall. Just before the first buildings turn sharp left and continue on the track to its end. Go through the waymarked wooden stile to the right and keep the wall on your left. At the end of the wall, 219 yards (200 metres) after the stile, turn right and cross field to a wooden stile in a fence. Cross the next field to another stile and the next field to the left-hand side of the castellated gatehouse of Endon Hall, where there is a stile into the lane.

5 Turn left along lane (Oak Lane) to the Macclesfield Canal ¼ mile (400 metres) away **D**. Cross the canal; descend the left-hand side of the crossover Bridge No. 29 and follow the towpath on the left-hand side of the canal for the next 1½ miles (2.4 km) to Bridge No. 26.

You will pass a marina on your right and the Adelphi Mill **E** with information centre on your left. Then cross Bollington Aqueduct. Here, leave the canal and turn left along road (take care with children as no pavement) and descend back to car park that is crossed by Middlewood Way viaduct **F**.

locks. It forms a part of the 97-mile (156-km) Cheshire Ring canal circuit. By the 1950s it was little used but with the restoration of the Peak Forest and Ashton canals the canal became used again and is today one of the most attractive skirting the base of the Pennine Hills. While walking along the canal Adelphi Mill **E** is passed. Built in 1856 it was

◄ A crossover bridge on the Macclesfield Canal, built to enable the horse pulling the boat to cross without unhitching.

originally a cotton mill but closed in the 1970s. The gatehouse is now an information centre.

The car park at the end of the walk is beside the Middlewood Way **F**. The way — 11 miles (18 km) long from Marple to Macclesfield — has been created from the former railway line, the M, B and M Railway (Macclesfield, Bollington and Macclesfield). The line opened in the 1860s and closed in 1970. In 1985 it was re-opened as a pedestrian, cycling and horse-riding route.

GOING FOR A BURTON

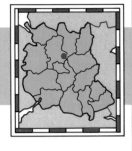

◀ *This splendid 19th-century bridge spans the River Trent at a point where there has long been a crossing. The wandering snail (inset) occurs in slow-moving waters such as the canal.*

SUE MORRIS. INSET: GEORGE BERNARD/NHPA

Discover the buildings and waterways of a famous brewing town

The all-pervading aroma of beer is the first thing that strikes the visitor to Burton upon Trent. Brewing has dominated this Staffordshire town for centuries, and the student of industrial history — as well as the beer enthusiast — will find much that is of interest here. In addition, some surprisingly green pockets remain, varying the scenery considerably in the compact area covered by this walk.

In the Middle Ages, the monks of Burton Abbey realized that the area's water, filtered through the local gypsum and rich in calcium and magnesium salts, was capable of producing excellent ale. Brewing continued in Burton after the abbey was dissolved. In 1744, William Worthington, a Leicestershire man, established a brewery in the High Street. William Bass did the same in 1777, and quickly established a reputation for fine quality beers.

Bass and Worthington were soon exporting their beers to the Baltic and Russia, and later to India. With the expansion of the railways in the 19th century, the Burton brewers began to exploit the home market, and beer became the national drink.

At the Bass Museum **Ⓐ**, where the walk starts, the visitor can learn all about the history and methods of brewing in Burton. Transport has always been an essential feature of the industry, and on display are early steam engines, vintage delivery vehicles and the Bass shire horses, which are still used to pull drays at shows and parades.

ROMAN WAY

The walk continues along busy streets. Derby Street follows the line of the Roman Ryknild Street (though it is difficult to picture this today), while Victoria Road is lined with 19th-century terraced cottages built for the brewery workers.

You turn off along the towpath of the Trent and Mersey Canal **Ⓑ**. Once busy with barges carrying cargoes of beer to the ports, the canal is now a leisure waterway. Colourful narrow boats glide along between the locks, and pleasure cruisers can be hired at

Shobnall Marina. The wild flowers by the water's edge, and the green expanse of Shobnall Fields opposite, provide a contrast with Burton's industrial face.

The route leads through St Paul's Square **Ⓒ**, now a conservation area, which was laid out following the building of St Paul's Church in 1874. The Gothic town hall was completed in 1894 by Michael Arthur Bass, the first Lord Burton. King Edward Place was created in 1906, after a visit by King Edward VII. Just around the corner in Wellington Street is a delightful row of almshouses, erected in 1875.

Some of the most significant buildings of Burton's industrial past line the next part of the route, which follows Borough Road and Station Street **Ⓓ**. The Midland Railway's

FACT FILE

- ☀ Burton upon Trent, 11 miles (17.6km) south-west of Derby, on the A38

- 🗺 Pathfinder 852 (SK 22/32), grid reference SK 249234

  miles 0 1 2 3 4 5 6 7 8 9 10 miles
  kms 0 1 2 3 4 5 6 7 8 9 10 11 12 13 14 15 kms

- 🕐 Allow 2 hours

- ▭ Level pavements and easy footpaths throughout

- P At the start. Pay & display parking at Union Street and Meadowside Leisure Centre

- T Well served by trains and buses. For details, and tourist
- I information, Tel. (01283) 516609

- 🏛 Numerous pubs, cafés and restaurants in Burton

- WC Bass Museum, main shopping centre, and Bridge Street

- 🏰 Bass Museum and Visitor Centre, Tel. (01283) 542031

THE WALK

BURTON UPON TRENT

The walk starts at the Bass Museum Ⓐ, in Horninglow Street.

1 From the main entrance to the museum, turn right along Horninglow Street. At the roundabout, turn left into Derby Street, and soon right into Victoria Road, which eventually becomes Dallow Road.

2 Just before the road crosses the canal Ⓑ, turn left down to the towpath. Continue, with the canal on your right, to Shobnall Marina. Walk up the steps to the road, and turn right (away from the canal).

3 Take the second left, Grange Street. Turn right down St Paul's Street. Walk around St Paul's

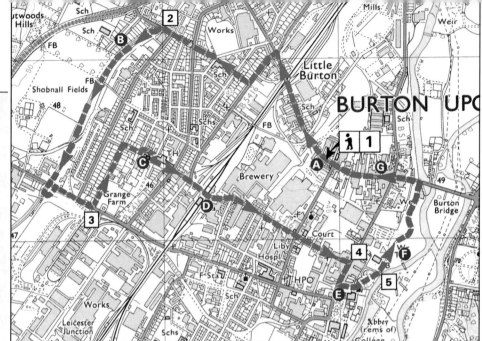

Square Ⓒ, and along King Edward Place, passing the town hall. Continue ahead across Wellington Street and down Borough Road, which becomes Station Street Ⓓ. Continue walking ahead, where the street is pedestrianized, to the High Street.

4 Turn right. At the Market Place Ⓔ, turn left. Go down the narrow lane to the left of the parish church. Take the path diagonally left across the Garden of Remembrance, towards the Washlands Town Park Ⓕ and the Andresey Bridge.

5 Just before the bridge, go through the gates on your left. Follow the path between the river and the town buildings to Burton Bridge. Climb to the bridge and turn left along Bridge Street, which becomes Horninglow Street Ⓖ, to return to the start.

Grain Warehouse No. 2 was built in 1854. Now restored for use as offices, it retains the 'crimson lake and cream' livery of the railway in its paintwork.

Across the railway line is the impressive Ind Coope Brewery, built in 1859. The elegant stuccoed building a little further on is the Ind Coope offices, built in 1865.

The massive Bass No. 2 Brewery, on your right, totally dominates the street. Inside the 3-foot (90-cm) thick walls is the famous Burton Union Room. Unions are containers in which fermentation of the beer is

▼These large barrels are unions for the final fermentation of beer. Behind them is the domed Magistrate's Court.

completed. The room, nearly a mile (1.6km) in length, held 2,548 unions (averaging four barrels each).

The Market Place Ⓔ contains the Parish Church of St Modwen, which stands on the site of the Benedictine abbey. The present church dates from a rebuilding in 1719, and has many monuments to brewers inside. The Victorian Market Hall is impressive, and the weekly Thursday market, originally granted by King John in 1210, is still held.

Beyond the Market Place is a delightful green area by the River Trent, the Washlands Town Park Ⓕ. It is possible to explore the island in the Trent by crossing one of the footbridges. The holy water from a chalybeate well on the island once

attracted many pilgrims to Burton.

The large watertower on the left was built in 1856 to store quantities of the precious Burton water, drawn up from wells for brewing. Further on, by the weir, is an impressive 32-arch bridge, built in 1864 to replace a medieval bridge. Burton has long been a strategic crossing point over the Trent. During the Civil War, Cavaliers and Roundheads fought almost incessantly for possession of the bridge, and Burton changed hands five times.

BRIDGE STREET

The last part of the route leads along Bridge Street and Horninglow Street Ⓖ. The Burton Bridge Brewery is one of a new wave of small breweries, and produces five different traditional cask beers.

Nunneley House was built in 1760 by Samuel Sketchley, and later occupied by Joseph Nunneley's brewery. The early 18th-century house nearby was Charles Leeson's brewery from 1753-1800. A number of other fine 18th-century houses, many of which are sadly in need of restoration, line the street on the way back to the Bass Museum.

SUE MORRIS

By Dogpole and Grope Lane

DEREK PRATT. INSET. NHPA

◀ *The first Tudor building you come to is Rowley's House, whose construction suggests it originally had an industrial use. The perch (inset) occurs in slow-moving sections of the Severn.*

FACT FILE

⚹ Shrewsbury

🗺 1:10,000 (SJ 41 SE), grid reference SJ 491129. A street map is recommended

miles 0 1 2 3   4   5   6   7   8   9 10 miles
kms 0 1 2 3 4 5 6 7 8 9 10 11 12 13 14 15 kms

◔ Allow 3 hours

▬ Mostly town walking. Suitable for all the family, though traffic can be heavy, especially on Saturdays. Sections along the river are muddy in winter

P Frankwell pay and display car park at the start

T BR Intercity; regular trains to and from the Midlands, Wales, London and the North-West

▦ Many pubs, restaurants and cafés in Shrewsbury

WC Riverside Shopping Centre, Bear Steps, Coleham Bridge

I Shrewsbury Castle and Rowley's House are open daily except on winter Sundays. For details of the abbey, Clive House Museum and Coleham Pumping Station, consult the Tourist Information Centre in The Square, Tel. (01743) 350761

A stroll in Shrewsbury, arguably England's finest Tudor town

The River Severn, swollen by rain from the Welsh mountains, loses its urgency when it reaches the Shropshire Plain. Any obstacle throws it into a meander. In Shrewsbury's case, the obstacle was a significant hill and the meander forms almost a complete circle.

The narrow neck of land that forms the break in this circle is reasonably high and easily defensible, making this an obvious site for a town. Possibly once a Welsh tribal capital, the town was certainly occupied by the Saxons, and by 1066 it was a significant town with five churches. After the invasion, it was fortified by Roger de Montgomery, the second richest and most powerful Norman after William I, who built a castle here.

FORTIFIED TOWN

The town and castle underwent further fortification until the Welsh were finally defeated, and Shrewsbury became a market town. It prospered in the Middle Ages and through into the reign of the Tudors.

Between 1560 and 1660, the town's population doubled. Much building work was undertaken, particularly of timber-framed mansions, and a good deal of the old town is still in evidence today. Besides the many fine buildings, there are ancient streets such as 'Doggepol' (today's Dogpole) and 'Le Wyle', both on record as early as 1246. Many interconnecting 'shuts' and passages, such as Grope Lane (1305), are also still in use.

The walk starts from the Frankwell car park, on the opposite bank of the Severn to the old town, and crosses the river at the Welsh Bridge Ⓐ. The present bridge was

THE WALK

SHREWSBURY

The walk starts in the Frankwell car park.

1 Go towards the river. Turn right along the bank to the Welsh Bridge **A**.

2 Cross and turn left to use the pelican crossing over Smithfield Road. Turn back to opposite the bridge, and then bear left into Hills Lane. Turn right to visit Rowley's House **B**. Return down Hills Lane, and go through the Victorian Shopping Arcade (opposite a car park) to the Mardol. Turn right to the entrance to Mardol Gardens opposite. Exit into Roushill.

3 Turn right to Roushill Bank, a pedestrian area, up past the entrance to Pride Hill Shopping Centre. This steep thoroughfare exits into Shoplatch. Turn left into Pride Hill's pedestrian area and carry on to Castle Street. Continue past Windsor Place on your right.

4 Turn left into School Gardens to pass the old school buildings **C**. Opposite Darwin's Statue, cross Castle Street to the half-timbered Castle Gates House and visit the castle **D**. Retrace your steps to Windsor Place. Enter Windsor Place and continue past St Mary's Church on your right and the Parade Shopping Arcade **E** on your left to St Mary's Court. This leads to Dogpole. Turn left and then right down a short

alley by an estate agents into St Alkmund's Square. Turn right and go round the church **F** to Bear Steps Hall **G**. Exit by Bear Steps and Grope Lane to the High Street. Turn right then left into The Square.

5 Leave The Square by the narrow Coffee House Passage to the left of the Music Hall. Continue to College Hill and the Clive House Museum **H**. Turn left, then right along the path through the churchyard to Belmont. Turn left, then right into Belmont Bank. Beyond Sycamore House, bear left into Barracks Passage. This exits into Wyle Cop and Henry Tudor House **J**.

6 Go down Wyle Cop and over the English Bridge

K, then continue straight ahead to the abbey **L**. Return to the English Bridge, but do not cross. Turn left to cross Rea Brook. Bear right to Longden Coleham, passing the Old Pumping House Museum **M**. At a pelican crossing, take a right turn to a footbridge back over the Severn. Turn immediately sharp left on a riverside path, and follow it for nearly 1 mile (1.6km) to the second bridge (a footbridge) back across the river. Cross to the Boathouse Inn. Turn right on a road, then right again into Water Lane. This returns you to the river. The riverside path goes under the Welsh Bridge to the Frankwell car park.

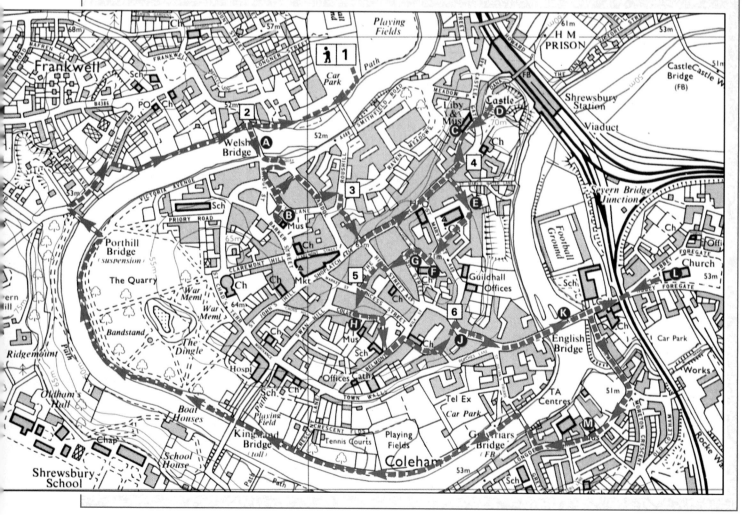

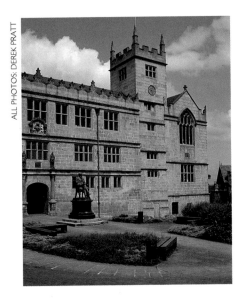

◄In front of the Old Grammar School, which now houses the town library, is a statue of its most famous old boy, Charles Darwin. Across the road is the 17th-century Castle Gates House (right).

completed in 1795, but earlier versions date back to 1155.

The first significant building on this route is Rowley's House ❸, off Hill's Lane. Now a museum, it has displays of Roman artefacts from nearby Wroxeter, and exhibits on Shrewsbury's medieval past. The building dates from the 1590s. The absence of chimneys suggests that it was probably originally used for processing wool rather than as a house. The adjoining Rowley's Mansion, built soon after, is the earliest brick building in the town.

The route continues through the Victorian Arcade to the Mardol, where there is a late 15th-century inn, the King's Head.

In School Gardens are the old buildings ❸ of Shrewsbury School, which date from the 1590s, although the school was founded by Edward VI in 1552. By the end of the 19th century, the school had outgrown the buildings and moved to a site

across the river at Kingsland. One of its best-known pupils was Charles Darwin, who was born at The Mount, near the start of this walk. The route leaves his statue to cross the road to Castle Gates House, built in the 17th century in the Dogpole, but moved to this site in 1702.

The gateway survives of de Montgomery's original castle ❹, but the remainder is the result of rebuilding by Edward I. Restoration was carried out by Thomas Telford at the end of the 18th century, and it was he who built Laura's Tower, worth climbing for the view. The Shropshire Regimental Museum is now housed in the castle.

ROYAL CONNECTIONS

In Castle Street is the Old Council House, where the Council of the Welsh Marches met until its abolition in the Civil War. Charles I and James II both stayed here. In Windsor Place, the route passes the 16th-century Perches Mansion and the 18th-century Windsor House, before reaching St Mary's Place. The Royal Salop Infirmary of 1826 has been reborn as the Parade Shopping Arcade ❺. St Mary's Court leads to the ancient Dogpole, which you

▼Shrewsbury Castle, built of red sandstone at the end of the 13th century and restored 500 years later, houses a military museum. The Bear Steps (right) are part of the medieval town.

cross to reach the church ❻ in St Alkmund's Square.

The tower is medieval, but the remainder of the fabric was rebuilt in 1793-95. This may not have been strictly necessary, but Old St Chads in the town collapsed as the clock struck four one morning in 1788. This panicked the nervous church authorities into rebuilding St Alkmund's as well. In Butchers Row, off the square, is the Abbot's House, and shop fronts that are little changed since the 15th century.

Bear Steps Hall ❼, dating from the 14th century and recently restored by the Civic Society, now

▲*English Bridge, which crosses the Severn on the eastern side of the town, was widened for traffic in 1925.*

stages exhibitions. The actual Bear Steps lead into Grope Lane, named in 1324 when it was a dark and narrow passage. This area, more than any other, retains the feel of medieval Shrewsbury.

The Square became the focal point of the town in 1292, when the market was moved here. The Market Hall, built in 1595, reflects the town's prosperity in the Tudor period. On the inside of one of the columns at the north end of the hall are some pegholes, which were once used to record sales of fleeces. At the far end of The Square is the Music Hall, built in 1839; also of note are Wooleys House (1730) and the 16th-century Plough Inn.

Coffee House Passage, by the Music Hall, takes you through to the Clive House Museum **O** on College Hill. Lord Clive, better known as Clive of India, lived in this house in 1762, when he was Mayor of Shrewsbury. The museum displays mostly porcelain and exhibits concerning life in the town during the 18th and 19th centuries.

Barracks Passage leads you to Wyle Cop, and Henry Tudor House **J**. Henry stayed here in August 1485 on his way to Bosworth, where he defeated Richard III and was crowned Henry VII on the battlefield. You pass Myttons Mansion and the Nag's Head Inn on the way to the English Bridge **K**, built in 1774, then dismantled and rebuilt in 1925 to widen the carriageway.

Gay Meadow, now Shrewsbury Town's football ground, is on your left. It is not unknown for the ball to be launched into the river during a game — on match days, one enterprising man patrols the river in a traditional coracle for the sole purpose of retrieving the ball.

BENEDICTINE MONASTERY

Just the other side of the bridge lies the abbey **L**. This Benedictine monastery, of which the Abbey Church is virtually all that remains today, was founded by Roger de Montgomery in 1080 on the site of a Saxon church. The refectory, cloisters and dormitory were once spread over the area where the main road now runs.

As you walk towards Coleham footbridge, you pass the Pumping Station **M**, which is now a museum. Its two large steam engines were built in 1900, and there are hopes of restoring them to full working order.

The return journey follows the riverside path around the outside of the town into The Quarry. The park is the site of an annual flower show. Standing in a commanding position at the top of the opposite bank is the main school building, originally a workhouse, of the present Shrewsbury School.

▼*The red-brick Coleham Pumping Station, built around the turn of the century, now houses a museum.*

Brother Cadfael

An illustration from A Rare Benedictine shows Brother Cadfael conducting inquiries.

No trip around Shrewsbury would be complete without some reference to Brother Cadfael. This fictional medieval sleuth is the creation of author and historian Edith Pargeter, who writes as Ellis Peters. She has given us a fascinating insight into life in 12th-century Shrewsbury.

Miss Pargeter was educated at Dawley and the County High School for Girls in Coalbrookdale. She began her working life as a chemist's assistant and joined the WRNS as a teleprinter operator in the war.

Her love for the area and her detailed historical knowlege of the period have combined to produce a credible character in a refreshingly different, but real setting. The Benedictine monasteries of the time held lands all over the country, and monastic business could take the brothers far and wide.

As a herbalist, Brother Cadfael had free licence to wander and to pursue his detective inclinations as he ministered to the sick away from his base in the abbey precincts. Much of the action, though, takes place around Shrewsbury itself.

The descriptions of places, and of the tension between the abbey and local people are based on fact; the abbey held the sole right for milling in the area until 1329, and this was a great bone of contention between the monks and the townsfolk.

Many of the places mentioned in this walk will be familiar to Cadfael fans, and details of a Cadfael Trail are available from the abbey, or from the Information Centre in The Square.

However, in 1766 the Grand Sluice **Ⓐ**, a sea lock, was built and river improvements began. Trade started up again. In 1884 a dock basin was opened up, and Boston is Lincolnshire's principal port to this day. All along the Witham, from the sluice to the Wash, fishing boats and other seagoing vessels are moored.

FAMOUS LANDMARK

Beside the river stands Boston's most famous landmark, and the focal point of the town, St Botolph's Church **Ⓑ**. It was begun in 1309. The octagonal tower, known as Boston Stump, was added in 1460. At 272 feet (83m), it is the tallest church tower in England. The 16th-century lantern on top acted as a beacon for travellers on land and sea. Visitors can climb the tower for a marvellous

◀ *St Botolph's soaring tower, ironically known as The Stump, dominates Boston. The small tortoiseshell and peacock butterflies (inset) love garden plants and are often seen around town.*

DEREK PRATT. INSET: STEPHEN DALTON/NHPA

A ramble around a historic town full of fascinating buildings

The ancient market town of Boston, on the River Witham, was a well-established port by the time of the Norman Conquest. By the end of the 13th century, it was second only to London. At this time there was a thriving trade route across the North Sea. Merchants came from all over to buy wool, salt and grain, and brought with them timber, wine and spices.

Boston was a centre of the wool trade and the town's fair was an international event. The notable Hansa merchants from Germany established a guildhouse in the town. When the wool trade slumped, Boston went into a sharp decline. The river silted up and the corporation petitioned that 'their borough might be put among the decayed towns'.

FACT FILE

- ✳ Boston, 14 miles (22km) north-east of Spalding, on the A16

- ▱ Pathfinder 816 (TF 24/34), grid reference TF 325445. A town map, such as the 1:10,000 used here, may be useful

  miles 0 1 2 3 4 5 6 7 8 9 10 miles
  kms 0 1 2 3 4 5 6 7 8 9 10 11 12 13 14 15 kms

- ◔ Allow 2 hours

- ▭ Town walk suitable for all the family

- P Long-term car park on corner of Norfolk St and Tunnard St

- T BR trains. Plentiful local and long-distance bus services

- Several pubs, cafés, restaurants and shops

- WC Market Place

- I Market takes place on Wednesdays and Saturdays. For tourist information, Tel. (01205) 356656

THE WALK

BOSTON

The walk begins at the long-stay car park on the corner of Norfolk Street (the A1137) and Tunnard Street.

1 Turn left out of the car park into Tunnard Street, and left again into Norfolk Street. At the end, turn right into Witham Place, then left over the Grand Sluice Bridge **A**. Turn left into Haven Bank. Walk along the bank of the River Witham to a footbridge just beyond St Botolph's Church **B**.

2 Cross the footbridge, and turn right into a cobbled alley with shops. This brings you out into Market Place at Fish Hill. Cross at the pedestrian crossing at the foot of a bridge. Continue following the road round to the right into South Street **C**. Cross by the Sam Newsom Music Centre, and go on to the traffic lights.

3 Go over a pedestrian crossing and turn left into John Adams Way for a few yards to the first right. The old Grammar School is to the right. Continue to the end of Rowley Road. A footpath leads to a bridge over Maud Foster Drain **D**.

4 Cross and turn left alongside the drain. Continue, crossing one road, to Bargate Bridge.

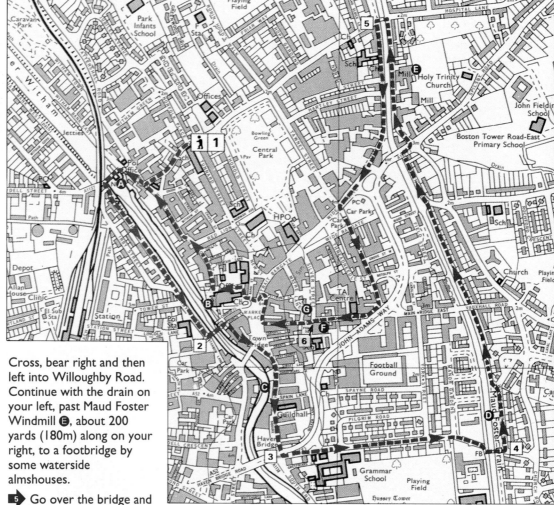

Cross, bear right and then left into Willoughby Road. Continue with the drain on your left, past Maud Foster Windmill **E**, about 200 yards (180m) along on your right, to a footbridge by some waterside almshouses.

5 Go over the bridge and left past Roper's Arms, along Horncastle Road to Bargate. Continue along the road to the traffic lights. Turn left over the pedestrian crossing and go straight down Pen Street. Follow a bend to the right at New Inn into Main Ridge West. Towards the end you pass the Masonic Hall **F** with its Egyptian facade.

6 Turn left into Pump Square and walk along the top of the square into Dolphin Lane. Look right up Mitre Lane to see Pescod Hall **G**. Turn right out of Dolphin Lane into Market Place. Go round Market Place, then bear right round St Botolph's. Turn right into Wormgate and continue straight up the road, which becomes Witham Place. By Boston Youth Centre, turn right into Norfolk Street to return to the car park.

view over a third of the county, including Lincoln Cathedral, 32 miles (51km) to the north-west.

Merchant guilds paid for the church, the interior of which is of cathedral-like proportions, with a high embossed roof supported by slender quatrefoil columns. The Jacobean oak pulpit was used by the

◄ *Boston's fortunes have risen and fallen with those of its port, which is on the tidal reaches of the Witham.*

non-conformist vicar John Cotton, who emigrated to Boston, Massachusetts (see box overleaf). Almost all the choir stalls are original, and have highly-carved misericords showing quaint subjects such as a bear playing the organ.

In front of the church is a statue of Herbert Ingram (1811-60) an MP for Boston and the founder of the *Illustrated London News*. He faces Market Place, where an open-air market with over 160 stalls is held on Wednesdays and Saturdays.

The walk continues past Town Bridge into South Street **C**, where many of Boston's best buildings are. Shodfriars Hall takes its name from the site of the old friary where it stands. Despite its authentic appearance, it is a Victorian copy of

ALL PHOTOS: DEREK PRATT

a 15th-century half-timbered building with decorative plasterwork.

In the early 14th century, Boston had four friaries. Little remains save for Blackfriars Hall, now an art centre. The Dominicans or Black Friars were the first to settle in Boston; the centre's facade is thought to have been their refectory wall.

Custom House Quay was the busy trading centre of the old port, which reached as far as St Botolph's. On the quay is Lincoln's Granary, built in 1741 — a brick shell containing a post and timber building. The

▲ *Boston's wealthy mercantile past is reflected both in substantial dwellings, such as the elegant Fydell House, and in handsome working buildings, like the tall Maud Foster Windmill (left).*

building is now the Sam Newsom Music Centre. There are other warehouses lining the river.

Boston's history can best be understood by a visit to the Guildhall Museum. Built in 1450, the Guildhall became the town hall a century later, and remained so for the next 300 years. The most interesting rooms are the prison cells where the Pilgrim Fathers were imprisoned and the Court Room where they were tried in 1607. The latter houses a display on John Foxe, the Protestant reformer who wrote *Foxe's Book of Martyrs*.

OLD MAYORAL HOME

Next door, in South Square, is Fydell House, a superb Georgian town house, built by a wealthy wine merchant who was three times mayor of Boston. It became the home of many generations of his family.

The route heads east to continue along Maud Foster Drain **D**, named for a 16th-century local landowner. It is part of a network of waterways built to drain the flat fenland and to provide a defence against the encroachment of the North Sea.

▶ *The Masonic Hall, in Main Ridge West, has an impressive 19th-century frontage built in the Egyptian style.*

The drains are navigable between May and September.

On the drain is another skyline landmark, Maud Foster Windmill **E**. With its seven floors, it is Britain's tallest working windmill. Its five whirling sails and ogee cap dominate the landscape.

Thomas and Isaac Reckitt built

◄Pescod Hall, a fine example of a 15th-century half-timbered house in Mitre Lane, has been carefully restored.

the cornmill in 1819. The brothers went bankrupt in the 1830s. Isaac later left for Hull, where he founded the business that was to make him a household name. Maud Foster is the only one of Boston's several windmills to survive. It has been restored by the Waterfield family and is open to the public, selling stoneground flour from a wholefood shop on the premises.

PESCOD HALL

You walk back into the medieval heart of Boston, passing the imposing Masonic Hall **F** on Main Ridge West. At the top of Mitre Lane is a lovely, timber-framed building, Pescod Hall **G**. From Market Place, the route goes along the intriguingly named Wormgate to return to the start.

▲Many of Boston's buildings show the influence of its trading partners across the North Sea, particularly Holland.

The Pilgrim Fathers

In the early 17th century, Boston became a centre of non-conformist religious views, inspired by a local man, John Foxe. In 1607, a group of Puritans, later known as the Pilgrim Fathers, tried to leave Boston illegally to seek religious freedom in Holland. They were betrayed by the ship's captain, and seven of their leaders were imprisoned in the Guildhall. A tablet above one of the cells commemorates two of them, William Brewster and William Bradford.

A month later they were brought to trial in the Guildhall Court Room. There was much public sympathy for them and they were eventually released. In 1608, they managed to reach Holland, and, in 1620, some of them formed part of the group of Pilgrim Fathers that sailed from Southampton in the *Mayflower*.

Ten years later, another band of Bostonians sailed to New England and founded the town of Boston, Massachusetts. John Cotton, the non-conformist vicar, became the first minister of the Christian Church, and Richard Bellingham the first

Governor of Massachusetts.

The connection between the two Bostons is very strong. The English town flies the Stars and Stripes on 4 July, Independence Day, and Fydell House has an American Room for the use of visitors from Massachusetts. When Boston Stump was in need of repairs in 1931, the American Bostonians donated £11,451 to its restoration.

In 1957, a memorial was erected to the Pilgrim Fathers, marking the point at Scotia Creek where they were arrested nearly 400 years ago.

Life was difficult in the early years for the first Pilgrim Fathers, who arrived in America in 1620. They and their families had to create settlements and farms out of the more-or-less virgin wilderness of the forests of New England. There they experienced winters more severe than those they were used to in their homeland.

Guthlac, as he became, had a reputation for holiness, and many people sought him out for spiritual counselling. One was Ethelbald, a pretender to the throne of Mercia.

ANCIENT PROPHECY

Fleeing from his cousin Coelred, Ethelbald sought sanctuary with Guthlac, who told him that one day he would become King of Mercia. Ethelbald said that if this prophecy came true he would build an abbey at Crowland. Ethelbald kept his promise and laid the foundations on St Bartholomew's Day.

Subsequent stone buildings on the site were destroyed by a fire in 1091 and by an earthquake in 1118.

◄The statue on Trinity Bridge may be of King Ethelbald. Henry VI landed here on a visit to the abbey in the 15th century. The common emerald damselfly (below) can be seen from June to September.

NEIL HOLMES. INSET: A.P. BARNES/NHPA

Visit an old abbey and a medieval bridge in the middle of the Fens

The town of Crowland, like Ely, March and Thorney, was once a low island in a sea of marshland. A small town grew up around an abbey, and was protected from flooding by great embankments. Drainage of the fens began in the 16th century but only when this was completed, in the 19th century, was Crowland safe from flooding.

The first abbey, founded in AD716, had wattle walls, a roof thatched with the local reeds and was supported by oak piles driven into the peat. It was built in honour of St Guthlac, a Benedictine monk who lived on the island for 15 years until his death in AD714.

Guthlac, the son of a Mercian nobleman, was a soldier, but gave up the military life to become a monk. He joined a monastery at Repton then sought a more secluded life on the island of Crowland. St

FACT FILE

✳	Crowland, off the A1073 6 miles (9.6km) north-east of Peterborough
os	Pathfinder 878 (TF 21/31), grid reference TF 241103

miles 0 1 2 3 4 5 6 7 8 9 10 miles
kms 0 1 2 3 4 5 6 7 8 9 10 11 12 13 14 15 kms

◕	Allow 1½ hours
▬	Flat walking on pavements and footpaths
P	Car park at the abbey
⊪	Several pubs, cafés and restaurants in Crowland

THE WALK

CROWLAND

The walk begins in the car park of the abbey **Ⓐ**, *signposted from the A1073.*

1 Go through the abbey churchyard, taking the left-hand path around the abbey. Turn left through the gate, then right along the road until you come to a footpath sign.

2 Turn right, keeping close to the abbey wall, then bear diagonally left over the park. Cross a bridge over a wide ditch and continue walking along the path to reach a main road (A1073).

3 Turn left and walk

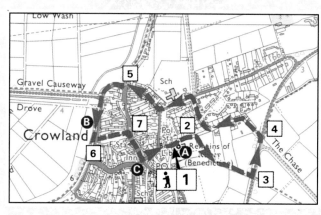

along the wide grass verge.

4 Turn left at the footpath sign. Go over a bridge and continue along a lane that curves to the left. Turn right into Church Lane. At a junction, turn left into Postland Road, then right into Kenny Street and continue until you reach a junction.

5 Take the higher path beside the old barns and cross to the right-hand side of the road. Continue walking along the pavement, with trees and views of the embankment **Ⓑ** and fens on your right.

6 Cross the road at the footpath sign on the opposite side. Go along this narrow path, part of which runs between fences.

7 Turn right into North Street then, at Trinity Bridge **Ⓒ**, turn left into East Street, keeping the war memorial on your left-hand side. Continue walking down the road, passing the library on your left, to return to the abbey car park at the starting point of the walk.

More rebuilding work was carried out in the 15th century. Much of the abbey survived the Dissolution of the Monasteries (1534), but was seriously damaged in the 17th century, during the Civil War, when Cromwell's cannons pounded the Royalist town of Crowland.

As the building decayed, stone was removed from the abbey by local people for building their houses. By the 19th century, what remained of the structure was in

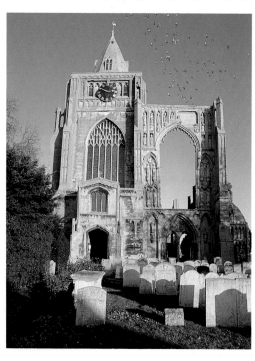

◀ The west face of the ruined Crowland Abbey, showing the parish church. Much of it dates from the 15th century.

▶ *To the west of Crowland the route follows an old flood bank alongside one of the ditches that drains the Fens.*

danger of collapse. A local clergyman launched an appeal that raised £3,000. This was enough to preserve the handsome ruin **Ⓓ** visible today, with its west front covered with statues of apostles, abbots, saints and kings. The north aisle has become the parish church.

The walk heads out over the Fens, with the abbey framed starkly behind you, then skirts around the northern edge of the old town.

FLOOD PROTECTION

At the western extreme of the route, you follow the course of one of the great banks **Ⓑ** that sheltered the town from the flooded marshland. Now drained, the peat soil successfully grows a variety of crops.

Returning to the centre of the town, you come to the 14th-century Trinity Bridge **Ⓒ**, a triangular structure with three arches. Before the Fens were drained, the streets of Crowland ran with water, and this bridge was constructed over the confluence of two streams, hence its unique shape. Too narrow for traffic

and too steep for horses, it is essentially a footbridge.

At the apex of the bridge there was once a large cross, traces of which can still be seen today. Because of the bridge's height and central position it was often used by preachers, and religious services are still held there today. It also made a good vantage point for the town crier's proclamations.

LEGENDARY STATUE

There are many legends about the origin of the statue on the bridge, but it is most likely that it was removed from the west front of the abbey early in the 18th century.

From the bridge, you return to the abbey through the old town, which, in 1226, was granted a royal charter for a market and a fair to be held annually at Bartholomewtide.

NORWICH CITY

NEIL HOLMES. INSET: PETER JOHNSON/NHPA

▲*On the banks of the River Wensum stands Pull's Ferry, a well-kept example of Norwich's medieval architecture. A member of the parsley family, giant hogweed (left) grows along roadsides.*

A walk through one of Britain's finest medieval cities

Three hundred years ago Norwich, one of England's largest provincial cities, was described as 'either a city in an orchard, or an orchard in a city, so equally are the houses and trees blended in it'. No industrial haze disturbed the view, nothing moved faster than a galloping horse or a passing swift and no noise came from the sky.

MEDIEVAL TREASURY

Today, Norwich remains a treasury of medieval Britain while providing services for an expanding industrial region. Remarkably, it is still a pleasant city in which to walk, its field paths, riverside walks and pedestrianized streets waiting to be explored. This walk covers the main centres of interest, while avoiding almost all of the traffic.

The car park in Britannia Road is a fine spot from which to view the city, and it also dispels the notion that all East Anglia is flat. It will be seen that Norwich — really an agglomeration of several medieval

FACT FILE

- ⚹ Norwich, 18 miles (29 km) west of Great Yarmouth, on the A11

- Pathfinder 903, (TG 20/30), grid reference 244093

  miles 0 1 2 3 4 5 6 7 8 9 10 miles
  kms 0 1 2 3 4 5 6 7 8 9 10 11 12 13 14 15 kms

- ◔ Allow 2 hours

- ▬ Elm Hill and steps up to the castle are steep

- P In front of Norwich prison on Britannia Road, on the edge of Mousehold Heath

- ¶ Numerous pubs, cafés and restaurants in the city

- WC By west door of cathedral. At the castle

- 🏰 Norwich Castle and its museum open daily, Tel. (01603) 223628 for times

TOWN WALKS

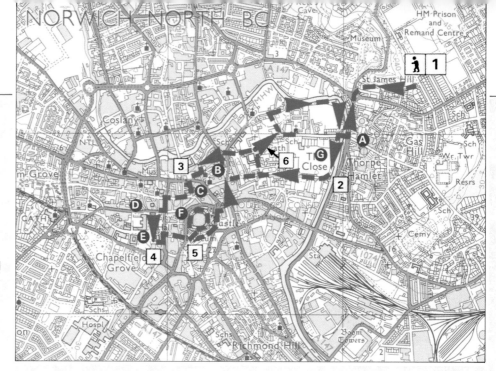

THE WALK

NORWICH CITY

The walk starts opposite Norwich Prison, in Britannia Road, which is off the B1140.

1 With the prison in front of you, turn right and walk along Britannia Road to a prominent belt of trees. Turn right here, taking a rough track and keep straight on to the Mottram Memorial. The path descends steeply left to the busy road. Cross the road to the pavement. Turn left, passing the Castle pub on your left. Cross a roundabout to the Lord Raglan in Bishop Bridge Road. After a short distance turn right across Bishop Bridge **A**. Cross the road to turn left along the Riverside Walk by a sign reading 'No cycles'.

2 Turn right here up to Lower Close and turn right at top of green to enter the cathedral under a coloured clock; the cloisters are on your left. Leave by the west door into upper close, passing through the main gate directly opposite. Cross the road at the pelican crossing. Turn right and take the second turning on the left up Elm Hill **B**. At the top turn left, then right into Princes Street. Continue straight on to reach St Andrew Street, opposite the square flint tower of St Andrew.

3 Cross the road at the pelican crossing, turn right and take first left up Bridewell Alley **C**. Turn right into Bedford Street ahead and left up Swan Lane. This leads into London Street. Turn right and keep right past Jarrolds Department Store on the corner. Cross Exchange Street. Ahead stands the chequered frontage of the Guildhall **D** (Tourist Information Office). Wander across the market and ahead rises St Peter Mancroft Church **E**. Take the steps beside the Sir Garnet Wolseley pub, turn right and skirt the church.

4 Bear left, and left again down Haymarket, passing a statue of Sir Thomas Browne on the right. Cross the road (now pedestrianized), turn left and look for the Royal Arcade on your right (when not open on Sundays, take the narrow street on the right before the arcade). Continue up Arcade Street. Ahead rises Castle Mound **F**, surmounted by its Norman keep. Cross the road at the crossing and turn right to ascend the flight of steps (steep and irregular) that curve round to the left. Views of the city can be gained by circling the foot of the castle walls.

5 Leave the keep by the same steps, turning left through Castle Gardens. Turn left passing dark-bricked Shire Hall, then right by the war memorial past Anglia Television. Turn left at the pelican crossing to go down King Street. The first turning on the right passes through Ethelbert Gate into Upper Close. Keep straight on past the statue of the Duke of Wellington on the left. Left at Lower Close towards the cathedral

again, bearing right at its door to pass the grave of Edith Cavell.

6 The path winds round, passing through an iron gate into Bishopgate. Cross the road to view St Helen's Church **G** and the Great Hospital. Retrace your steps along Bishopgate, then bear right along it. At the next corner bear right again, passing the Adam and Eve pub and taking a path straight through its car park towards the river. Keep right along this wooded walk beside the River Wensum which passes Cow Tower. Keep right at the road to run onto Bishop Bridge. Cross it, turn left to return to the roundabout and keep left, passing the Lord Raglan and Castle inns. Retrace your steps to the prison and the start of the walk.

---

villages — straddles the River Wensum, while tucked within a wide bend of the River Yare. The magnificent panorama ahead is dominated by the cathedral and, appearing almost behind its spire, the green patina-topped bell-tower of the city hall. To the left, the panelled tower of St Peter Mancroft **E**, a true city church, rises elegantly,

while to the right, nearer the horizon, stands the square-towered bulk of St John's Roman Catholic church.

Bishop Bridge **A**, built in 1340, is the only surviving medieval bridge in the city. Nearby is Pull's Ferry, dating from the reign of Elizabeth I. A plaque under the archway and a notice board on the river bank explain its significance. From here

beautiful houses frame a quiet back street, once the canal along which building materials were hauled to the cathedral. Set serenely in a slight hollow, Lower Close reveals the magnificent southern elevation of the cathedral soaring cliff-like above neat lawns and the largest cloisters in England. This cathedral must have one of the cleanest

▲ *The exquisite vaulting in the nave adds to Norwich Cathedral's reputation as one of the finest in the country.*

with local artefacts. Beyond, at number three, is the Mustard Shop, where beautifully displayed and presented examples of this local product make useful souvenirs.

FINE CHURCHES

Notice the flush flintwork of the Guildhall **D**, now a tourist information office. Close by, the largest open-air market in England is fronted by St Peter Mancroft and its clear glass clerestory windows. St Peter's, one of the many city churches, is much used, polished and lovingly upkept by the people of Norwich. Its hammer-beam roof is masked by false vaulting, below which the east window filters sunlight through 15th-century Norwich glass.

NORWICH CASTLE

With its magnificent external decoration, Castle Keep **F** dates from 1160 and is an outstanding example of Norman military architecture. Today it houses an equally outstanding museum and art gallery with, in particular, an excellent display of landscape pictures by the Norwich School of Artists. These pictures were avidly collected by

exteriors in the land, its external stonework revealing rich colouring, enhanced by a pastel clockface over the entrance.

Leave by the west door and pass the precincts of Upper Close, where Admiral Nelson attended school, before passing through the gateway, built five and a half centuries ago by Sir Thomas Erpingham, knight at Agincourt, and characterized in Shakespeare's *King Henry V.*

COBBLED STREETS

Elm Hill **B** is a restored medieval street, its cobbled surface rising steadily between irregularly placed frontages of vernacular architecture. St Andrew's and Blackfriars were once vast monastery churches. Nearby, in Magdalen Street, is Gurney Court, once the home of Elizabeth Fry (1780-1845), Quaker and prison reformer.

Bridewell Alley **C** houses the Bridewell Museum, which is packed

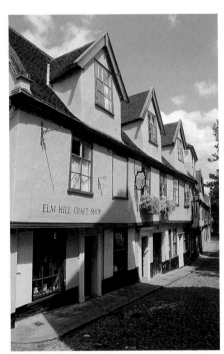

▲ *Its cobblestones and well-preserved shop frontages make Elm Hill one of the city's most attractive streets. Colman's Mustard Shop in neighbouring Bridewell Alley (right) was opened to mark the firm's 150th anniversary.*

ALL PHOTOS NEIL HOLMES

Nature Walk

When your walk takes place in a city, watch out for any clues as to its history, especially in areas which have been left untouched.

THE CORN EXCHANGE, where corn was traded, is often a grandiose building usually situated close to the village market place.

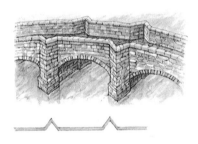

PASSING PLACE BRIDGES date from the days before motor cars. Their purpose was to enable pedestrians to avoid oncoming carriages.

RICHARD PHIPPS

THE MUSTARD SHOP

wealthy local families in the early 19th century.

Two squat towers above Castle Gardens mark the spot where, in days gone by, convicted criminals were publicly executed, to the huge delight of crowds in the cattle market below. Robert Kett, who led a peasants' rising in 1549, died here, hanged from the castle walls.

The 700-year-old flush flint archway of Ethelbert Gate takes you out of the rush of the city, into the

For a short distance, the route follows the banks of the River Wensum, an oasis of peace in a busy city. The Royal Arcade (bottom left) was recently renovated to its true Art Nouveau splendour.

ALL PHOTOS NEIL HOLMES

serenity of Cathedral Close, which contains beautiful houses, some Georgian, some earlier, several of which have now been turned into offices. Just past the cathedral door lies the grave of Edith Cavell, a heroic nurse, who was executed by the Germans in 1915 for helping British prisoners escape.

THE GREAT HOSPITAL

The flint tower of the parish church of St Helen **G** marks the entrance to the Great Hospital, founded in 1249 and still being built. Access to the church is through the gardens, via a cloister, where enquiries at reasonable hours will produce a key.

St Helen's was once larger, but during the Reformation much of it was divided into communal wards where the sick and elderly took shelter. Notice the colourful ceiling of the Lady Chapel and Elizabethan Commandment Boards. A final stroll along the banks of the Wensum leads back to the start.

The Norwich School

The Norwich Society of Artists was formed in 1803, at a time when the city had something of a national reputation as a centre of radical political thought. Its 30 or so members met to sketch mostly local scenery, discuss technique and display their work annually.

Two notable members were John Crome (1768-1821) and John Sell Cotman (1782-1842). Crome, the founder of the society, was also its leading artistic personality. Without any formal training, other than that received as an apprentice coach and sign painter, he developed a sturdy and individual style.

His work was recognized by Thomas Harvey, a wealthy Norwich weaver, who enabled Crome to widen his perspective across his varied collection of landscape paintings. None of his early work before his mid-thirties survives. He later found patronage with the powerful Gurney family. His work was ranked by his contemporaries alongside that of Constable and Turner.

Crome had complete mastery of aerial perspective. This was the result of acute observation and a developing technique of sketching outdoors in oils. Although he maintained a clear distinction between this and his finished work in the studio, he suffered many plagiarists and copyists.

John Sell Cotman was the son of a tradesman. He moved to London at the age of 16, where for eight years he was very successful, winning prizes, exhibiting at the Royal Academy, and was ranked by his contemporaries alongside Turner. Then, at 21, he returned to Norwich and became a prominent member of the society. However, his move was followed by a series of unfortunate events, including false patronage, which finally led to profound frustration and embitterment.

Although a superb oil painter, he is best remembered for his consummate skills as a topographical water colourist and architectural draughtsman. He immortalized the varied buildings of the Norfolk scene, as Crome did with the trees, spacious marshes and glinting broads.

Norwich Market Place, a water colour painting by John Sell Cotman, is today seen as one of the prominent examples of the Norwich Society of Artists, formed in the early 19th century.

TATE GALLERY

for its increased activity. Addressing a public meeting in the town in 1843, he promised that he could build a railway to take fish from the port straight to Manchester.

In 1847 this promise became a reality and the town expanded rapidly on the silver back of the herring. At the height of the season, 700 herring boats sailed from Lowestoft, carrying 1,500 miles (2,400km) of drift nets. Teams of fisher girls came from the Highlands of Scotland every year to take jobs in the town gutting and packing the catch.

All this activity inevitably led to overfishing, and the drifters are now gone. They have been replaced by trawlers that fish all year round up

◄*There has been a lighthouse at Lowestoft for over 300 years, since Britain's first was built here. This one was built in 1874. Kittiwakes (inset) have taken to nesting on buildings.*

NEIL HOLMES. INSET: SWIFT PICTURE LIBRARY

FACT FILE

✳ Lowestoft, Suffolk

🚉 Pathfinder 925 (TM 49/59), grid reference TM 542915

miles 0 1 2 3 4 5 6 7 8 9 10 miles
kms 0 1 2 3 4 5 6 7 8 9 10 11 12 13 14 15 kms

◔ Allow 2 hours

▬ Pavements, parks, promenades, sea walls and sandy beaches

Ⓣ Well served by buses and trains

Ⓟ In road at start of walk

🏛 Numerous pubs, cafés, restaurants and shops in Lowestoft

Ⓘ Tourist Information Office at the harbour

A stroll around Lowestoft, Britain's easternmost town

Lowestoft has much to offer the visitor. There is clean, safe sea-bathing off South Beach, a busy fishing and commercial port and interesting buildings in the ancient streets of the old town.

The walk begins above South Beach and heads north to the harbour, which you cross via Town Bridge Ⓐ. The bridge is frequently raised for sea traffic, separating the town on these occasions into two areas of mutual frustration, but if you are in no hurry you can relax and watch the activity in the inner and outer harbours.

Lowestoft was not always such a bustling port. Sir Samuel Peto, the contractor who built Nelson's Column, was the man responsible

▶*Lowestoft is a busy commercial port and fishing harbour. Boats come down the River Waveney, passing under Town Bridge to the North Sea.*

NEIL HOLMES

THE WALK

LOWESTOFT

The walk begins from Rectory Road by the South Beach. Approach along the A12 from the south. After the A1145 joins from the left take the third turning on the right, which is signposted 'South Beach'.

1 Walk towards the sea and then turn left to walk along the cliff top, which slopes down past Claremont Pier and the Tourist Information Office towards the harbour.

2 At South Basin bear left past the Royal Norfolk and Suffolk Yacht Club, then right to cross Town Bridge **A**. Go right down Waveney Road and left into Battery Green Road alongside Waveney Dock **B**. Turn right down Hamilton Road and, at its end, steps give access over the sea wall to a walkway. Turn left. Ahead, by the 7th groyne, is the most easterly point in Britain,

Lowestoft Ness **C**.

3 Where the walkway ends, continue along the beach until you reach the next flight of steps up the sea wall. Climb these and head for a white lighthouse rising out of some trees. Cross Whaplode Road, and turn right to reach the entrance to Sparrow's Nest Park and the cottage maritime museum **D**.

4 Follow winding woodland paths to the highest part of the park, exiting onto the road at the top of Cart Score **E**.

5 Cross the road to explore Belle Vue Park, a good spot for a picnic, then leave by the same entrance and return to town past the lighthouse **F**. The High Street **G** begins at the Royal Falcon pub. At the junction by The Wheatsheaf pub bear right down London Road North, which soon becomes pedestrianized.

6 The 'Call of the Sea' statue points you towards Town Bridge. Cross it and retrace your steps to the start; as a minor variation, you can return along the firm sand at the water's edge, past Claremont Pier.

to 400 miles (640km) out into the North Sea, catching plaice, cod, dogfish, brill, halibut and sole.

From Town Bridge the walk goes down by Waveney Dock **B**, where the fish are landed. Brightly painted fishing boats vie for your attention with the chandler's shops and tattoo parlours that line the streets.

The next part of the walk takes you along the sea wall past Lowestoft Ness **C**, the most easterly point in Britain. The spot is not marked, and is usually deserted. Kittiwakes have built their deep, cup-shaped nests on a vast frozen food complex nearby, as well as on buildings near Town Bridge. These dainty gulls first started nesting here in 1958, and this is one of only a handful of breeding colonies on the east coast.

MARITIME MUSEUM

Beyond the Ness, the route heads inland again to Sparrow's Nest Park, where there is a small maritime museum **D**. You go through this park to Belle Vue Park, and just inside the entrance are the Beacon Stones, which date from 1550, and a notice explaining their significance.

The two parks are separated by Cart Score **E** ('score' is the local name for a narrow lane, usually one connecting a road to the beach). This was once the site of the town gallows. Slightly downhill, you come to the lighthouse **F**, built in 1874.

◄Regularly split by wooden groynes, the sands at South Beach are popular with bathers in the summer.

This is the successor to Britain's first recorded lighthouse, sited here in 1676, when Samuel Pepys was Secretary to the Admiralty.

The High Street **G** begins at the Royal Falcon. This was formerly North Flint House, built around 1551, and home to two prominent local families. Crown House, nearby, was the home of Sir James Smith, founder of the Linnaean Society.

Just beyond the squat-towered town hall stands another 16th-century inn, The Crown, while the handsome, knapped-flint South Flint House is of a similar date. No. 83 housed Samuel Pacey, a noted 17th-century witch-hunter.

The pedestrianized London Road North, where a modern shopping arcade is named after Sir Benjamin Britten, Lowestoft's most famous son, leads back to Town Bridge. From here you can either retrace your steps along the cliff or go along the beach to the start.

NEIL HOLMES

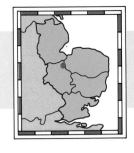

◄*North Brink has some fine Georgian and Victorian buildings, including several designed by Algernon Peckover, who lived at Peckover House. The dot moth (inset) is common in summer.*

changed course, but the draining of the Fens, and the consequent rise in agricultural production from the early 18th century, made Wisbech a prominent trading and shipping centre once again. This new wealth financed the splendid Georgian houses that now grace the town.

This walk begins at the Parish Church of St Peter and St Paul **A**. The size of this large, dark church reflects a period of prosperity. The nave has four aisles, one of them Norman. An unusual feature is the separate tower, built about 1520.

Thomas de Braunstone (died 1401), a constable of Wisbech Castle, is commemorated by a splendid brass in the chancel, while Matthias Taylor, a 17th-century constable, has a fine carved stone memorial. Above the south porch is the room where Wisbech Grammar School was founded in the 15th century.

A back lane by an old, red-brick wall leads to Alexandra Road and the Angles Centre **B**, a theatre and arts complex housed in a Georgian

Historic treasures and fine buildings round a riverside town

Wisbech is one of the architectural gems of East Anglia and deserves to be better known. Until recently, a certain unkemptness and lack of care veiled the appearance of the town, and although there are still plenty of buildings in need of restoration, there is a general movement towards improving and upgrading the old areas of the town, so that Wisbech is now emerging from its chrysalis of age and decay.

The town has a long history. In the Middle Ages, the sea came within a mile or two, and Wisbech was one of the main ports on the Wash. King John lost his jewels and baggage here in 1216, not further out in the Wash as is often thought.

The fortunes of the port waxed and waned as rivers silted up or

▲*Octavia Hill's birthplace on South Brink. A lifelong housing reformer, she also helped found the National Trust.*

FACT FILE

⁕ Wisbech, 12 miles (19.2km) south-west of King's Lynn, off the A47

▱ Pathfinder 899 (TF 40/50), grid reference TF 463095. A street map, such as the OS 1:10000 used here, is useful

miles 0   1   2   3   4   5   6   7   8   9   10 miles
kms 0   1 2 3 4 5 6 7 8 9 10 11 12 13 14 15 kms

◔ Allow 1 hour

▭ Town walk on pavements and paths. Suitable for all the family

P Car park near the start

T For information regarding BR services from Peterborough, Tel. (01733) 68181

⑂ Several pubs, hotels, cafés and restaurants in Wisbech

WC In the car park at the start and on Chapel Road

⌂ Peckover House (National Trust), Tel. (01945) 583463. Wisbech and Fenland Museum, Tel. (01945) 583817

I Tourist Information Centre at the library, Tel. (01945) 583263

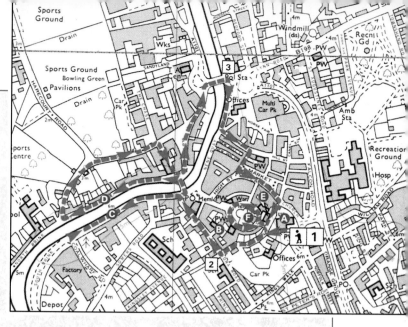

THE WALK

WISBECH

The walk starts outside the Parish Church of St Peter and St Paul Ⓐ.

▶1 Walk through the churchyard, with the main door of the church to your right and a garden for the blind on your left, to Love Lane. Follow this alleyway left and continue ahead where it opens out.

▶2 At a T-junction, turn right into Alexandra Road and follow it past the Angles Centre Ⓑ. Turn left along South Brink Ⓒ to Coal Wharf Road. Retrace your steps to the Town

Bridge. Turn left over the bridge and walk along North Brink Ⓓ. Turn sharp right along Chapel Road to the Old Market. Turn right and walk around three sides of the market before continuing right along the main road, now North Street. Bear right to cross Freedom Bridge.

▶3 Turn immediately right along Nene Quay. Turn left up Hill Street, then right near the Old Grammar School, to the Market Place. Turn left and go through the market square back towards the church.

Turn right beyond the tower, and go straight along the path down the side of the Wisbech and Fenland Museum Ⓔ on your right. Turn right up the steps beyond its main

entrance towards The Castle Ⓕ. Beyond the Library and Information Centre, go right and continue walking around The Crescent to return to the church.

▲ *The museum has a series of etchings that show Wisbech in its heyday.*

theatre, built in 1793. It is the second oldest theatre still in use in England, and the great actors Edmund Kean and William Macready played here.

The walk continues along the Brinks, which Nicholas Pevsner described as 'one of the most perfect Georgian streets of England'. The Georgian terraces on South Brink Ⓒ include the birthplace of Octavia Hill, the housing reformer, and the Old Grammar School (one of two in the town) near the end of the street.

HOUSE AND GARDEN

North Brink Ⓓ, on the other side of the River Nene, is even more splendid. Elegant Peckover House, formerly known as Bank House, was home to the Peckover family for 150 years, then given to the National Trust in 1943.

Built in 1722, the house has a rather restrained exterior, but an outstanding interior, with excellent decorative wood-carving, panelling and plasterwork. It is furnished in contemporary style, and suitable paintings have been lent or donated.

The walled Victorian garden is also worth a visit. It contains many fine plants, including a maidenhair tree and a tulip tree, and there is a lovely collection of roses. In the conservatory are orange trees that are thought to be 300 years old. There is also an 18th-century stable block, housing a collection of harnesses, and a 16th-century barn.

ANCIENT TIMBERS

Next on the route are the Old Market and the present Market Place, which superseded it in the early 13th century. The Old Market is now characterized by several substantial buildings, most of them Georgian and early Victorian. Some had ancient warehouses at the back, by the river, but many were washed away during floods, notably in 1978.

The present Market Place has a complete mixture of buildings. The Rose and Crown pub has a pretty courtyard linking its different parts of varying ages; underneath are early Tudor barrel vaults. Off New Inn Yard, at the end of Market Place, is the oldest vernacular building in Wisbech, a timber-framed barn or

boathouse of around 1500.

A little further on you will find the Wisbech and Fenland Museum Ⓔ, which was founded in 1835 by a group of eminent local people, including William Peckover and his younger brother, Algernon, who donated the first exhibits. Soon the rented accommodation became overcrowded. This led to a move to purchase land and erect a purpose-built museum in 1845.

The museum became well known and attracted some important gifts, among which was the manuscript of Charles Dickens's *Great Expectations*. The museum went through a period of decline early in the 20th century, but its fortunes have since revived and its exhibitions now combine displays connected with fenland and local life with antiquities of worldwide interest.

The early 19th-century houses of The Crescent were built by Joseph Medworth. Central to the scheme is The Castle Ⓕ, built by Medworth for himself in 1816. This replaced a grand house built on the site of a Norman castle in 1658 by Thurloe, secretary to Oliver Cromwell.

The gate piers are from the original mansion. The moat of the Norman castle has contributed to the layout of the later town and has caused a certain amount of subsidence in some of the buildings, including the museum.

SHIP OF THE FENS

DENNIS MANSELL. INSET: L. CAMPBELL/NHPA

FACT FILE

- Ely, Cambridgeshire, just off the A10

- Pathfinders 941 (TL 48/58) and 961 (TL 47/57), grid reference TL 544798

  miles 0 1 2 3 4 5 6 7 8 9 10 miles
  kms 0 1 2 3 4 5 6 7 8 9 10 11 12 13 14 15 kms

- Allow 2½ hours plus plenty of time for visits

- Along streets, walkways and well-maintained footpaths

- In Ship Lane and other car parks around the city

- A wide choice of shops, pubs, cafés and restaurants in Ely

- Cathedral: Mon-Sat, 7am-7pm, summer; 7.30am-6pm, winter. Admission charge. Sun 7am (7.30am, winter)-5pm. Stained Glass Museum open daily, March-October. Ely Museum, High Street: Tues-Sun, Tel. (01353) 666655 for times Oliver Cromwell's House (Exhibition): summer, 10am-6pm, daily; winter (1 October-1 April), 10am-5.15pm. Closed Sun

◀Masons currently engaged in the restoration of this magnificent Romanesque cathedral have found the stone piers in perfect order. In summer, the bright meadow buttercup (inset) carpets the Fenland fields in gold.

A pleasant walk to discover Ely and its surrounding countryside

The charm of Ely, one of Britain's smallest cities, is enhanced by the green spaces, which extend right up to the cathedral walls. The surprise is the relative steepness of its thoroughfares, here in the heart of the Fens, and its jewel is the Cathedral Church of the Holy and Undivided Trinity, dominated by a magnificent west tower and eclipsed by its octagon — the most daring and original architectural achievement of the Middle Ages. This walk also explores many of the city's medieval buildings and samples its magnificent fenland setting.

On leaving the car park, the walk takes you back along Broad Street to the castellated entrance of The Park. The path uphill to Cherry Hill gives fine views of the Cathedral **❶**, framed by mature trees. Notice in particular the west tower, which has stood here for 800 years, and the unique octagonal wooden lantern, erected in the early 14th century when the cathedral's central Norman tower collapsed.

To carry out this undertaking in timber was a structural achievement of the first magnitude in the English Middle Ages. For 12 years England was scoured for oaks of sufficient faultless scantling; some 21 yards (20 metres) long by 1 yard (1 metre) square. The transportation of the timber demanded that roads and bridges be strengthened from as far

THE WALK

AROUND ELY

Approaching Ely from London or Cambridge along the A10, take the A142, Angel Drove, to the east. At the next roundabout turn left, then first right along Broad Street, to the 'free parking' sign on the right in Ship Lane where the walk begins.

1 Leave the car park and retrace your steps to Broad Street. At Broad Street cross the road, turn left and walk on until you reach the castellated entrance to The Park on your right.

2 Follow the path uphill to Cherry Hill through The Park, noting the fine views of the Cathedral **H** on your right. Continue to the end of The Park — about 300 yards (270 metres) to see the huge Monks' Granary barn **A** on your left.

3 After leaving The Park continue straight ahead towards the Porta **B**. Do not pass through it but turn right and detour for

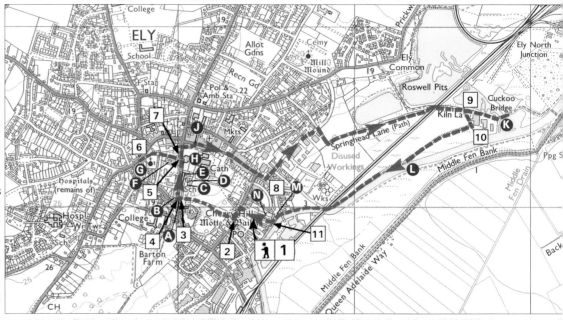

just over 100 yards (90 metres) down a shaded walk to visit Prior Crauden's Chapel **C**. Retrace your steps back to the Porta.

4 Go through the Porta to reach The Gallery and immediately cross over and turn right. Walk along the

Gallery, which affords excellent views of the Cathedral, passing the Headmaster's House (Queen's Hall) **D** and the Bishop's House (Great Hall) **E** on your right. After almost 300 yards (270 metres) you will arrive at Palace Green,

with the Bishop's Palace **F** on your left.

5 Turn left and make for the cannon in the centre of the Green for another fine view of the Cathedral. With your back to the Cathedral, walk through the Green, straight ahead to reach Oliver Cromwell's

▲*Ely Porta was originally the gate that led to the medieval Benedictine monastery and the riverside buildings.*

as Hatfield Forest and Chicksands in Bedfordshire, and today 400 tons of lead-covered wood hangs, seemingly in space, held by timbers reaching to eight stone pillars.

ROYAL CONNECTIONS

As you leave Cherry Hill, look to the left to see the huge Monks' Granary Barn **A**. Dating from the same period as the cathedral, it is used as a dining hall by the King's School. The school has associations with more than one king; founded by Alfred the Great, Edward the Confessor received his early education at the Benedictine Abbey, while Henry VIII refounded the School in 1543. King's occupies many of the city's medieval domestic buildings.

Ahead stands the Porta **B**, originally the main gateway to the Benedictine Abbey. Before passing through it, detour down a shaded walk to enjoy Prior Crauden's Chapel **C**. Tiny, 14th-century and

beautifully maintained, it exudes a quality of peace only to be found in an English cathedral close.

Returning to the Porta, pass through it to walk along The Gallery, which offers more excellent views, from across the road, of the west tower and octagon over ancient roofs, with Prior Crauden's Chapel to the rear. Pass the Houses of the Headmaster (the Queen's Hall) **D** and the Bishop (the Great Hall) **E**, on the right, on the way to Palace Green, with the Bishop's Palace **F**, part early-Tudor and partly in the Wren style, on the left.

LADY CHAPEL

Stand by the cannon in the centre of the green for a further celebrated view, this time of the west front of the cathedral, and to the left the largest Lady Chapel in England. Built detached as an aisle-less hall in 1321 by Alan of Walsingham, it was completed just before the advent of

House **G**, abutting St Mary's Churchyard.

6 Retrace your steps back across the Palace Green to visit the Cathedral.

7 On leaving the Cathedral turn right and then right again into Steeple Row until you reach Steeple Gate **J** on your left. Pass through this into the High Street and turn right along it for 200 yards (180 metres) to arrive at the market-place on your left. Continue straight ahead into Fore Hill for 350 yards (315 metres) until you reach Lisle Lane on your left.

8 Turn left into Lisle Lane and continue for 450 yards (405 metres) until arriving at a footpath signposted 'Hereward Way', which curves to form a beautiful, tree-lined walk. Continue on this path until you reach a level crossing. Cross it and continue down the path to just inside the fence.

9 Continue straight on down through a National Rivers Authority yard to Cuckoo Bridge **K** — an excellent site for wildfowl. Retrace your steps back to the fence, pass through a kissing gate on the left and reach a raised causeway leading across rough pastureland to arrive at the riverbank after about 100 yards (90 metres).

10 Turn right and walk along the bank of the River Ouse **L** for just over ½ mile (800 metres) to reach a railway bridge on the right. Go under the bridge and continue along the willow-lined Riverside Walk for 250 yards (235 metres) until you come to a footbridge. Go over the bridge and, still keeping to the riverbank, continue past an extremely thin 'Ladder House' **M** on the right to reach Ship Lane.

11 Turn right into Ship Lane, go past The Maltings **N** on your right and return to the car park, also on your right. Alternatively, continue straight on down Riverside Walk to visit the Cutter Inn for some much-needed refreshment before returning to the car park.

◀The Norman nave, with its Victorian painted ceiling has undergone much restoration over the years and is now a truly glorious sight.

▶Hereward Way footpath is named after Hereward the Wake, the Fenland rebel who took refuge from William the Conqueror on the Isle of Ely.

the Black Death in 1349.

Ahead, abutting the churchyard of St Mary's Parish Church is the former home of Oliver Cromwell and his family **G** for 11 years from 1636. Cromwell rose to power during the English Civil Wars to become Lord Protector of the Commonwealth during England's brief period as a republic.

Ely, (Eel Island), owes its religious and commercial existence to St Etheldreda, an East Anglian princess, who, in 673, having escaped two unhappy marriages (while still retaining her virginity) fled from her second husband to become a nun here on lands bequeathed from her first marriage. The religious house was subsequently sacked by Danish invaders, but somehow the candle of Christianity flickered on and, in 1083, Abbot Simeon, then in his eighties, was despatched to this remote island to commence the present building, larger and more magnificent than anything before, both to glorify God and to enhance the prestige of the Benedictines.

In 1109 Ely was made a Bishop's see, and the First Bishop secured the privilege of an annual fair of seven days, to which was given the name St Etheldreda's (St Audrey's) Fair.

ELY MARKET

Following the Thirty Years War, Cambridge became the only place for discharging ships inland on the Great Ouse, and Ely had to content itself with lighter merchandise, such as laces and trinkets. It is from these small and inexpensive stuffs sold at St Audrey's Fair that we get the word 'tawdry'.

The 16th-century Steeple Gate **J**

Oliver Cromwell

Oliver Cromwell, the Lord Protector of the Commonwealth, lived in Ely for 11 years with his wife and family of eight children.

Oliver Cromwell, the English soldier and statesman who led the parliamentary forces in the Civil Wars, came to Ely in 1636 when he was 37 years old. Son of a rootedly Protestant family of declining fortune, he had married the daughter of a prosperous London merchant 16 years earlier. But, with a growing family to support, he was sliding down the social scale; from landowner at Huntingdon, to grazier at St Ives. Now his uncle had died and Cromwell arrived in Ely to become a landowner once more.

Whatever his financial position, he undoubtedly belonged to the English ruling classes and was related to almost every family of importance in the country. His was also a parliamentary family and as soon as he took his seat in the House of Commons, at the age of 29, he began his angry, relentless attacks against the rulers of the Church.

By his 40th birthday, Cromwell was established as a man of substance, taking an active part in town life and was a recognized spokesman for the Puritans in the eastern counties, as well as a champion of the Fenland men.

This was the time of the 'Adventurers', who adventured their capital in a scheme to drain the fens, turning them into 'good summer land' within six years. The Fen people naturally opposed an undertaking that would change their way of life and deny them their living from fishing and wild fowling. They were also unimpressed by the thought of earning wages from other men in return for drainage work. Cromwell successfully opposed the action of the Earl of Bedford's company, which tried to claim the land as the reward before completing the work. He did, however, agree with the principle of fen drainage and eventually reappointed the Dutch engineer Vermuyden to complete the work.

Cromwell combined qualities of leadership with a hatred of all ritualism. He was sufficiently confident to present himself at the cathedral in 1643, lock the door and pocket the keys. The building remained closed for 17 years. In 1646, he became the first chairman of the Council of State of the new republic after the execution of Charles I and moved to London. At the end of 1653, Cromwell took the oath as Lord Protector of the Commonwealth of England. A year later he addressed his first parliament, which he dissolved in 1655. He remained Lord Protector until his death in 1658.

▲*The walk along the willow-lined banks of the gently flowing River Great Ouse gives a fine view of The Maltings.*

(1.6 km) out past Ely station, pause at the top of Stuntney Hill. Behind is the finest view of the 'Ship of the Fens', as the cathedral is known locally, set in some of the richest agricultural land in Britain.

▼*From across the flat expanse of the Fenland, the magnificent cathedral does indeed look like a galleon in full sail.*

leads to the High Street and, on the way to the market place, Ely Museum has many interesting exhibits of this fenland city and the story of its people.

From the city, 'Hereward Way' leads out towards the River Ouse, curving to form a beautiful tree-lined walk. The end of this lane holds a haven — Cuckoo Bridge **Ⓚ**. The reed and sedge banks of this quiet backwater support a wide variety of waterfowl.

A raised causeway across rough pasture soon leads to the banks of the River Great Ouse **Ⓛ**. Here you can follow the willow-lined riverside walk and return to Ship Lane, passing the extremely thin 'Ladder House' **Ⓜ** and The Maltings **Ⓝ**.

Leaving Ely it is worth taking the A142 Newmarket road. Just 1 mile

NEIL HOLMES. INSET: NATURE PHOTOGRAPHERS LTD

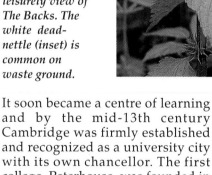

▲*Punting is a favourite pastime on the Cam and provides a leisurely view of The Backs. The white dead-nettle (inset) is common on waste ground.*

Walking around a famous and historic university city

The mellow stone and brick buildings of the university colleges, with their rolling lawns and weeping willows on the river banks, provide the setting for this walk through Cambridge, one of England's top tourist attractions.

However, Cambridge was an important market town long before the university was established. The earliest known settlement in this area dates from Roman times, and what today is the market place was once the site of Saxon settlements. In 1068, shortly after their famous Conquest, the Normans built a castle near the old Roman site. According to the Domesday Book, there were about 400 houses in Cambridge by 1086.

Cambridge first came to prominence in 1209, when a number of scholars moved here from Oxford.

FACT FILE

* ✴ Cambridge

* 🆑 Pathfinder 1004 (TL 45/55), grid reference TL 449584

  miles 0 1 2 3 4 5 6 7 8 9 10 miles
  kms 0 1 2 3 4 5 6 7 8 9 10 11 12 13 14 15 kms

* 🕐 Allow a minimum of 3 hours

* ▭ Walking on pavements and tarmac paths

* P Multi-storey car parks in Lion Yard, Park Street and Queen Anne Terrace. Park and ride sites in Clifton Road (south) and Cowley Road (north)

* T BR main line service

* 🍴 Plenty of cafés, pubs and restaurants

* WC Lion Yard car park, Silver Street, Jesus Green, Midsummer Common, Christ's Pieces, Parker's Piece

* I Information Office at back of Guildhall

It soon became a centre of learning and by the mid-13th century Cambridge was firmly established and recognized as a university city with its own chancellor. The first college, Peterhouse, was founded in 1284 by the Bishop of Ely and, in the next two centuries, 11 more colleges were founded. Today the university has around 10,000 undergraduates, and some 30 colleges.

The walk starts at the Guildhall, opposite the colourful stalls of the market place, and soon you pass the University Church of Great St Mary's. Just across King's Parade are the administrative headquarters of the university **Ⓐ**.

THE WALK

CAMBRIDGE

The walk starts in the city centre, in front of the Guildhall.

1 Facing Market Hill, make for St Mary's Passage, to your left. Follow it to King's Parade. Turn left, noting the university's administrative headquarters **A** behind and to your right. Continue past King's College Chapel.

2 Turn right down Silver Street and continue until you reach the river, from where there is a view of the Mathematical Bridge **B** and Queens' College. Return along the opposite side of the road. On your right are the Anchor pub, a mill pool and the University Graduate Centre. Turn right into Laundress Lane. At the end of the lane, turn right and cross the river. Turn left alongside the river, with the Old Granary at Darwin College on your right.

3 After 140 yards (130m), take the tarmac path to your right. After crossing two footbridges, turn right to go between an old mill building and another mill pool.

4 At Newnham Road, turn right. At the traffic lights, go straight on and continue along Queen's Road for about 500 yards (450m), with

Queens' College and The Backs **C** to your right. Just beyond the back gate to King's College, fork right onto a gravel path. To your right there is a fine view of King's College Chapel.

5 At a wooden railing, turn right into Garret Hostel Lane. When you reach a bridge **D**, there are fine views in both directions. Proceed past Clare College on your right. Turn left onto Trinity Lane, then follow

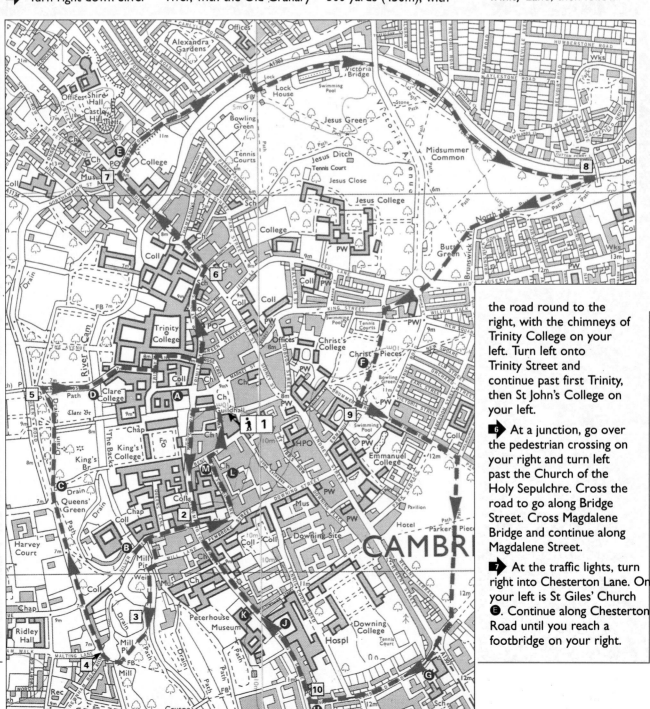

the road round to the right, with the chimneys of Trinity College on your left. Turn left onto Trinity Street and continue past first Trinity, then St John's College on your left.

6 At a junction, go over the pedestrian crossing on your right and turn left past the Church of the Holy Sepulchre. Cross the road to go along Bridge Street. Cross Magdalene Bridge and continue along Magdalene Street.

7 At the traffic lights, turn right into Chesterton Lane. On your left is St Giles' Church **E**. Continue along Chesterton Road until you reach a footbridge on your right.

Cross it to reach Jesus Green. Turn sharp left and follow the towpath. Go under the road bridge, or go up some steps and cross Victoria Avenue via two pelican crossings to your left. Either way, you come to Midsummer Common. Continue along the towpath, going under the footbridge at the Fort St George pub.

8 At the next footbridge (Cutter Ferry), turn very sharp right and take the next path to your right across the common. When you come to Maid's Causeway, near a roundabout, cross the road, turn right and cross Short Street. Go forwards into King Street. Take the first left into Pike's Walk to cross Christ's Pieces **F**.

9 At the entrance to the bus station, turn left along the pavement. Go straight on across Emmanuel Road and continue along Parker Street. At the traffic lights, cross to the other side and continue for 80 yards

(70m). Turn right onto a tarmac path that leads you diagonally across Parker's Piece. Cross Regent Terrace and bear right along the pavement, opposite the large Roman Catholic church. Cross Regent Street and go ahead down Lensfield Road, with the Scott Polar Research Institute **G** and, further on, Hobson's Conduit **H** on your left.

10 At a T-junction, turn right into Trumpington Street. Continue past Old Addenbrooke's Hospital **J** and Fitzwilliam Museum **K**, then past Peterhouse College on your left and Pembroke on your right. Turn right into Botolph Lane, with St Botolph's Church on your left. Take the next turn left onto Free School Lane, passing the old Cavendish Laboratory **L**. Turn right into Bene't Street, noting St Bene't's Church **M** to your left. Turn left onto Peas Hill and then turn right to bring you back to the front of the Guildhall.

▲ *The Mathematical Bridge was so called because, based on geometric principles, it was constructed without nails or bolts. The Church of the Holy Sepulchre (below right) is of 12th-century origin.*

framed in weeping willows, and, to the south, to Clare and King's. You may even be tempted to try your hand at punting — there are several points along the river from which you may embark. Just over the bridge stands Trinity Hall (1350), whose gardens are famed for their herbaceous borders.

The Church of the Holy Sepulchre, just beyond Trinity and St John's, Cambridge's two largest colleges, is something of a rarity. It is one of only four round churches in the entire country.

There are three colleges on King's Parade. The first on the route is King's, founded in 1440 and housing a magnificent pinnacled chapel. This is sometimes open to the public

and well worth a visit. Next is the early red brick of St Catherine's, built in 1473 and, over the road, the grey stone of Corpus Christi, which predates it by over a century.

Down by the river is Queens' College, founded in 1448. The famous Mathematical Bridge **B** connects the two parts of the college. Originally constructed in 1749, it was rebuilt in 1902.

Soon you come to one of the aesthetic highlights of the walk, an area known as 'The Backs' **C**, where trees and graceful lawns slope gently down to the river behind east-facing college buildings.

At Garret Hostel Bridge **D** pause to look to the north to Trinity Bridge,

◄*Trinity, the largest, richest and grandest college, was founded by Henry VIII in 1546.*

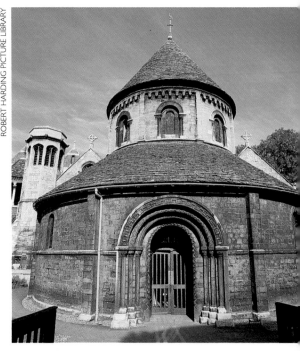

Magdalene (pronounced 'maudlin') Bridge stands near the old Roman site and is the 'bridge' from which the city takes its name.

At St Giles' Church **E** it is possible to take rubbings of the fine brasses found within, while nearby, housed in what was formerly the White Horse Inn, is an interesting Folk Museum.

MEDIEVAL FAIR

As you walk alongside the river, you skirt the edge of Midsummer Common, where one of the largest fairs in the country has been held since the Middle Ages. Soon you cross Christ's Pieces **F**, a delightful small green area with a wonderful display of flower beds in spring and summer. Parker's Piece is larger and accommodates several cricket and hockey pitches.

On Lensfield Road is the Scott Polar Research Institute **G** which was founded as a memorial to Captain Scott and his companions.

Further along the road is Hobson's Conduit **H**, originally located in the market place, and the outlet for the city centre's first drinking-water supply. The water came from springs about three miles

▲*Hobson's Conduit is named after the carrier Thomas Hobson (1544-1631), a well-known figure in his day.*

(5km) away. Hobson, a carrier, was one of several people involved in the project, and is immortalized in the phrase 'Hobson's Choice', meaning no choice at all. He had about 40 horses for hire, but refused to let out any horse except the one which had rested for longest!

Old Addenbrooke's Hospital **J**, no longer used for its original purpose, was founded with money left by John Addenbrooke, a graduate of St Catherine's College, and opened in 1766. The Fitzwilliam Museum **K**, one of the best outside London, was founded in 1816 with a bequest from the 7th Viscount Fitzwilliam. It houses several important collections. Just past the museum is Peterhouse, the oldest college. On the other side of the road is Pembroke (1347); its chapel was the first building designed by Sir Christopher Wren.

ATOMIC RESEARCH

Further on, in Free School Lane, the old Cavendish Laboratory **L** was founded by the 7th Duke of Devonshire, and it was here that Lord Rutherford did his early work on splitting the atom and other experiments which led to the development of nuclear physics.

The Saxon Tower of St Bene't's Church **M** (the name is an abbreviation of St Benedict) is the oldest surviving building in the city, and was probably built in about 1025; the main church building is of a somewhat later date.

▼*The Scott Polar Research Institute contains relics of Captain Robert Scott's Antarctic expeditions.*

The University and the Colleges

The university is actually a body of people ('The Chancellor, Masters and Scholars'), governed by selected members known as the Regent House. The role of the university is to teach, hold examinations, confer degrees and conduct research.

The central administration of the university is concentrated at The Old Schools building. Next door is the Senate House, where the Regent House meets and where degree certificates are presented.

The colleges provide undergraduates with board and lodging. Each college is separate and controls its own affairs, and most were established by a wealthy patron. The oldest is Peterhouse, founded in 1284 by Hugh de Balsham, Bishop of Ely; the newest is Robinson founded in 1977 by David Robinson who made his money from television rentals.

Each college has tutors called Fellows, who provide tuition to small groups of students, which supplements university lectures by concentrating on essay writing and reading. To be accepted by the university as an undergraduate, a student must also gain admittance to a college. Initially, each college catered only for a single sex, but now almost all are mixed.

The Old Court at Corpus Christi College, which was founded by the townspeople of Cambridge in 1352.

HILLS OF CROYDON

An unexpectedly rural walk in the heart of a London suburb

The London Borough of Croydon, which has grown enormously this century with the overspill population from the metropolis, may seem an unlikely spot for a rural ramble. The route passes through green surroundings for well over half its distance, and most of the remainder is on footpaths through residential areas.

The circular route takes in some very attractive woodland and parkland scenery, a splendid ridge walk, a nature reserve and a beautiful landscaped garden.

VIEWS OVER LONDON

The walk begins at South Croydon Station, in the heart of a residential area. However, suburban development soon gives way to the woodland of Croham Hurst. The spine of the woods is the whaleback hump of Breakneck Hill **A**, the site of a prehistoric settlement. The path

MARK CRICK. INSET: VIC COBBOLD/SWIFT PICTURE LIBRARY

▲*Coombe Wood, below Addington Hills, has lovely, landscaped gardens. The edible oyster mushroom (inset) can be found from autumn to spring on both living trees and fallen timber.*

FACT FILE

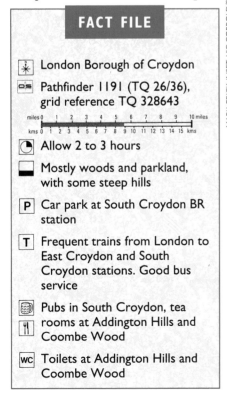

✳ London Borough of Croydon

🗺 Pathfinder 1191 (TQ 26/36), grid reference TQ 328643

miles 0	1	2	3	4	5	6	7	8	9	10 miles
kms 0	1 2 3	4 5	6 7	8 9	10 11	12 13	14 15	kms		

🕐 Allow 2 to 3 hours

▬ Mostly woods and parkland, with some steep hills

🅿 Car park at South Croydon BR station

🚆 Frequent trains from London to East Croydon and South Croydon stations. Good bus service

🍴 Pubs in South Croydon, tea rooms at Addington Hills and Coombe Wood

🚻 Toilets at Addington Hills and Coombe Wood

---

goes along the crest of its ridge, which rises to 472 feet (144m) and offers views in several directions.

On the other side of Littleheath Woods **B** is Bramley Bank Nature Reserve **C**, run by the London Wildlife Trust. It has five species of amphibians and interesting flowers.

Addington Hills **D** are a haven of woodland and rough grassland. On a clear day, there is a panorama right across London, to the Chilterns in the west and Epping Forest in the east. Major landmarks are clearly identified on a viewing platform.

The route descends into Coombe Wood **E**, where there is a fine landscaped garden and a cafeteria where the Chinese proprietors calculate your bill on an abacus.

Finally, the walk follows the Vanguard Way, a long-distance path, through Lloyd Park **F**, before heading back to South Croydon. Lloyd Park was once farmland but, in 1927, was presented to Croydon Corporation in memory of the landowner, Frank Lloyd.

THE WALK

CROYDON

The walk begins at South Croydon BR station.

1 Turn left beside the forecourt and descend the long flight of steps to the road. Turn left. In 150 yards (140m) cross and turn right up Moreton Road. Pass Doveton Road to bear left; then, where Moreton Road bears right under the bridge, go left up the steps and keep ahead to cross a footbridge over the disused railway line. Follow the path, bearing right onto the road, then pass a school and bear left to the major road. Cross, then follow the footpath ahead, until you reach Croham Manor Road.

2 Cross to the grassy area at the entrance to Croham Hurst. Turn right by the bench seat, and enter a wood on a wide path rising gently. After 100 yards (90m), bear left up a steep gravel path to reach the open, grassy ridge of Breakneck Hill **A**. Follow the ridge for 700 yards (630m); about halfway along divert to the right on the spur for a better view, then return to the main path. At the end of the ridge, descend steeply, bearing right to join the road.

3 Cross and turn left along the pavement for 400 yards (360m), then cross back over and turn left along Queenhill Road, crossing a major road and a T-junction, and going ahead up some steps into Littleheath Woods **B**.

4 Keep ahead on a narrow path for 80 yards (75m), then turn left along a wider path to an open, grassy area. Turn right along the edge of an open

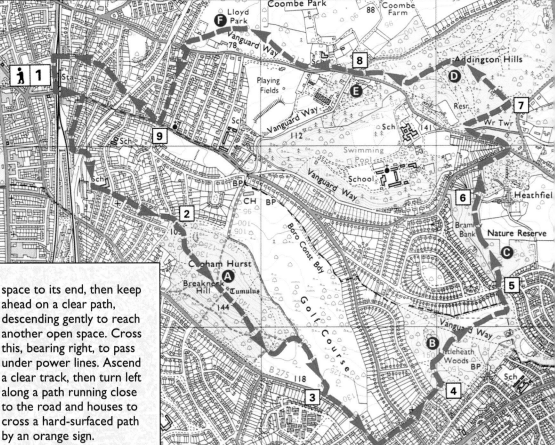

space to its end, then keep ahead on a clear path, descending gently to reach another open space. Cross this, bearing right, to pass under power lines. Ascend a clear track, then turn left along a path running close to the road and houses to cross a hard-surfaced path by an orange sign.

5 Go half-right across the grass to a fence, beneath a sign 'London Wildlife Trust : Bramley Bank Nature Reserve' **C**. Take the left-hand entrance and follow the main path ahead. Fork right to follow a series of short, white-topped posts. At the end of the bank, descend to the corner of a field fence. Keep ahead beside the fence, to the road, where there is a reserve information board.

6 Follow the road ahead to the T-junction. Turn right to the main road, then turn left to cross it on a zebra crossing and follow the dirt track beside it. Cross a minor road and turn right on a path through woods. After 50 yards (45m) turn right on the major track to the car park and driveway at the

main entrance to Addington Hills **D**.

7 Turn left along the driveway past a Chinese restaurant to the viewing platform. Go down a steep gully to the left of the platform, turn right at the bottom, then left. Go straight ahead to the T-junction of paths just 20 yards (18m) from the road and turn right. Follow the path to the car park by the junction of Oaks Road and Coombe Lane. Almost opposite is the entrance to Coombe Wood **E**.

8 Go along the right-hand pavement of Coombe Road to a large open space (Lloyd Park **F**). Follow a grassy path half-right away from the road for some distance, then bear left to a

children's playground beside a bomb crater. Keep ahead in the same direction, to the right of a large brick pavilion, then between the tennis courts and the bowling green to Lloyd Park Avenue. Turn left to the main road. Cross it and turn left then immediately right up a bridleway, to a road.

9 Turn right, then right again into Campden Road, and almost immediately left along a footpath. Follow the footpath across a road, then over a footbridge (across a disused railway line) and another three roads, to reach the bridge over the main railway line. Cross and turn sharp left through a gap in the wall, to follow the footpath back to the station.

A ROYAL PARK

heath. In 1497, it was the scene of King Henry VII's victory over Michael Joseph's Cornish rebels.

Next to the heath lies the Royal Park. It was enclosed in 1433 by Henry VI and later walled by James I. Its present design dates from 1662, when Charles II commissioned the French designer André Le Nôtre to produce plans for a formal layout of the site. Unfortunately, Le Nôtre never visited Greenwich and failed to take account of the steep escarpment dividing the park.

◀ *The gracious 17th-century buildings seen from the park include the Queen's House, designed by Inigo Jones, in the foreground with the twin cupolas of the Royal Naval College behind. The grey squirrel (inset) can be seen in the park.*

PHILLIP CRAVEN/ROBERT HARDING PICTURE LIBRARY. INSET: T & G COLEMAN/AQUILA

FACT FILE

✳ Greenwich, 6 miles (9 km) east of Charing Cross

▱ Pathfinder 1175 (TQ 27/37), grid reference TQ 395762

miles 0 1 2 3 4 5 6 7 8 9 10 miles
kms 0 1 2 3 4 5 6 7 8 9 10 11 12 13 14 15 kms

◕ Allow 4 hours including visits to historic sites

▭ Easy, level paths

P In Blackheath and Greenwich Park. Very little parking in Greenwich itself at weekends

T BR stations in Blackheath, Greenwich, Maze Hill. Boat service: see Greenwich Pier for times and destinations. Regular bus service (53) into Central London

▦ Numerous cafés and pubs on the route of the walk

WC Next to main top gates, at the Old Royal Observatory and next to the Cutty Sark

⌂ Old Royal Observatory, National Maritime Museum, The Queen's House, *Cutty Sark*; admission charge for all. Day passport and family ticket

A London walk, rich in naval history and architectural interest

Greenwich is famous as the centre from which world time is measured. Lying on a bend in the River Thames 5 miles (8 km) downstream from the centre of London, it has a unique history. Settled by Romans, later used as a raiding base by Vikings, it was the birthplace of Henry VIII and a favoured residence of English monarchs for over two centuries.

The walk starts on the heath above Greenwich at the Neo-Gothic All Saints Church. In pre-Roman times paths ran down from the heath to the Thames below. The Romans built a road across the heath, connecting London with Dover and Canterbury.

HISTORY OF THE HEATH

Blackheath's proximity to London and commanding views made it strategically important. In 1011, the Viking army encamped there and later, both Wat Tyler's Peasant Army, in 1381, and Jack Cade's Rebels, in 1450, petitioned the King from the

THE WALK

BLACKHEATH – GREENWICH PARK – GREENWICH

The walk begins at the main (north) entrance to All Saints Church, All Saints Drive, Blackheath.

1 Walk north across the heath towards Greenwich Park Gate Lodge, which is visible from the church. (Use Canary Wharf Tower as a marker — the point of the Tower rises above the main Shooters Hill Road by the pelican crossing.) Enter park through main gates.

2 Follow the avenue straight ahead. After 400 yards (360 metres) the road swings left. Carry straight on to the statue of General Wolfe and the viewing area **A**.

3 Left of the statue is the Old Royal Observatory **B**. Follow the path alongside the Observatory through the iron kissing gate. Cross the East-West Longitude line and continue down to the road. Turn right and follow the railings downhill. After 150 yards (135 metres) follow the railings round to the right away from the road. Continue diagonally right across the park. After 140 yards (126 metres) the path narrows. Continue for another 250 yards (225 metres) and leave the park by the pedestrian gates next to the Maritime Museum **C**.

4 Enter the grounds of the Maritime Museum through gates on the immediate left. Turn left and follow the path past the entrance to the Museum. Continue for 200 yards (180 metres) then re-enter the park by the gate on the left opposite the museum café. Turn right and follow the path to the main bottom gates. Leave park and take the first turning on the left (Nevada Street). At the end of Nevada Street, turn right and follow the road round into Greenwich High Road. St Alphege Church **D** is on the left. Cross at the zebra crossing to the railings of the church.

5 Bear right and continue for a few paces, then cross at the zebra crossing where Creek Road intersects on the left and carry on straight ahead. The Tourist Information Centre is across the road on the right-hand side. Continue on to the pedestrian concourse where the *Cutty Sark* **E** and the *Gypsy Moth IV* are in dry dock.

6 Take the path that runs alongside Greenwich Pier with the Thames on the left. Continue past the Naval College **F** to the Trafalgar Tavern **G** on Park Row. Take the alley that runs behind the Trafalgar Tavern and past the front of the Yacht Tavern to Trinity Hospital **H** and Greenwich Power Station.

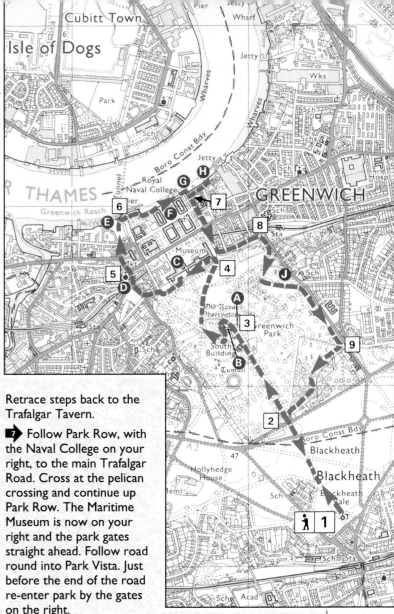

Retrace steps back to the Trafalgar Tavern.

7 Follow Park Row, with the Naval College on your right, to the main Trafalgar Road. Cross at the pelican crossing and continue up Park Row. The Maritime Museum is now on your right and the park gates straight ahead. Follow road round into Park Vista. Just before the end of the road re-enter park by the gates on the right.

8 Take the left-hand path until the corner, then cut right across the grass to a flight of steps. Climb steps and continue to the top of the hill where three paths meet. Take the left-hand path, ignoring the right-hand path that runs down a steep hill. Ahead and to the left is Vanbrugh Castle **J**. Continue until a number of paths meet. Follow the path to the right running alongside the park wall for 400 yards (360 metres).

Where the path turns sharp right, enter the Flower Gardens by the gate ahead on the right.

9 Follow the path ahead for 250 yards (225 metres). In front of the pond take the left-hand path and continue round the garden to the gate. Leave the gardens and turn left for the main top entrance to the park. Return to All Saints Church across the heath.

Instead of the central tree-lined avenue leading up to the Queen's House, it actually leads to the edge of a 100-foot (30.5-metre) drop.

This oversight, however, provides the modern visitor with unparalleled views over London. From the viewing area **A**, St Paul's Cathedral, the Docklands developments and the great sweep of the River Thames through London are all visible.

The Old Royal Observatory **B** next to the viewing area was commissioned by Charles II and designed by Christopher Wren. Built in 1675, on the site of an old Watch Tower, there have been a number of additions to Wren's original design.

The Observatory later moved to Sussex and is now in Cambridge. The Greenwich buildings these days house an exhibition of scientific instruments and a planetarium. On one wall of the Observatory is the GMT 24-hour clock and nearby a line on the path showing the Greenwich Meridian. There cannot

▲The statue of General Wolfe beside the Old Royal Observatory, built in 1675 and designed by Christopher Wren.

be many walks in this country that allow you to stand with a foot in each hemisphere.

In 1894 there was an attempt to blow up the Observatory — but the bomb exploded prematurely, killing the carrier. It was this incident that inspired Joseph Conrad's classic story, *The Secret Agent*.

THE QUEEN'S HOUSE

The Maritime Museum **C** contains the finest collection of naval artefacts in the country. At the centre of the museum is the Queen's House. It was built as a gift from James I to his wife, Queen Anne, although it was not completed until the reign of Charles I. Designed by Inigo Jones, it is one of the finest examples of his work, drawing heavily on the Italian Villa style with simple lines and little outward decoration.

The work of another great English architect is well represented in Greenwich. Nicholas Hawksmoor was commissioned to provide a new parish church after a great storm in 1710 destroyed the old one. He built St Alphege **D** on the supposed site of the martyrdom of Archbishop Alphege by the Danes in 1012. The many famous people who have attended the church have their names recorded on plaques and tombstones. Across from the church is the covered market, which holds a Craft Fair at weekends.

TEA CLIPPER

The *Cutty Sark* **E** is perhaps Greenwich's best known landmark. The last surviving clipper ship, she sits in dry dock overlooking the Thames. Built in 1869 on the Clyde, the *Cutty Sark* could reach a speed of over 17 knots and cover 360 miles (576 km) a day. Originally built for the tea trade, she made her name as a wool clipper sailing back and

forth to Australia. Alongside the *Cutty Sark* lies *Gypsy Moth IV* sailed by Sir Francis Chichester. Although dwarfed by its famous neighbour the *Gypsy Moth* was in fact the largest single-handed yacht ever built when it was completed in 1966.

RIVERSIDE SITE

Just downstream is the Royal Naval College **F**. The site it occupies is one of the most historic locations in Greenwich: the original foundations of the Royal Palace of Placentia. The Palace was used by the English Monarchy from 1447 until the Restoration. It fell into disrepair during the interregnum and was pulled down by Charles II. The King had grand plans for the riverside site, but his grandiose designs were never realized. A notoriously fickle monarch, Charles lost interest in the project and only the King Charles building was completed.

It was not until the reign of William and Mary — who granted a charter for the foundation of a Royal Hospital for Seamen in 1694 — that work re-started on the site, this time under the direction of Sir Christopher Wren. From the outset, however, great restrictions were placed on his design. Queen Mary insisted he maintain a line of sight from the Queen's House to the Thames. Wren was left with little choice but to create an avenue

◄A detail of the architectural elegance of the Queen's House. The design by Inigo Jones was his first major work and was based on the principles of the Italian architect Palladio.

▼A three-masted tea-clipper, the Cutty Sark *was famous in its day as the fastest ship of its type. Launched in 1869, it was berthed in Greenwich in 1957.*

Henry VIII in Greenwich

During the reign of Henry VIII (1509-1547) Greenwich enjoyed its heyday as a Royal residence. Henry was born and grew up in the Palace of Placentia on the banks of the River Thames. When he became king his court was often in residence at Greenwich.

Henry would hawk and hunt in the Royal Park and inspect his ships on the Thames. His passion for shipbuilding led him to establish new shipyards nearby. He also built an armoury at Greenwich, bringing in German craftsmen to create fine suits of armour.

Henry's court was more European in style than anything England had seen before. There were masques, dances and banquets often attended by hundreds of guests. Henry was a keen sportsman and Greenwich Park witnessed numerous jousts and tournaments, many of which Henry competed in himself. One of the most splendid occasions must have been the reception given to Emperor Charles V who arrived at Greenwich in a procession of 30 barges, bringing with him a retinue of 2,000.

Despite the pageantry, Greenwich was also the scene of some of Henry's darker moods. The arrest of Anne Boleyn's brother and friends was at a tournament in Greenwich Park. Later, King Henry signed her death warrant at the Palace of Placentia and she was beheaded on 19th May 1536.

Greenwich Palace from the Thames, the birthplace of Henry VIII in 1491. The site is now the Royal Naval College

▲*The Queen's House flanked by the Royal Naval College. Designed by Wren, the college was commissioned by William and Mary as a naval hospital.*

elderly. Next to the hospital is the massive Greenwich Power Station, built in 1906 to provide London's then-growing tram network with electricity. These days it is used as a back-up power supply for the London Underground.

VANBRUGH CASTLE

The path leading to Vanbrugh Castle ❿ has excellent views back over the Power Station and across the Thames to the East End of London. Vanbrugh Castle lies just outside the walls of the park. Sir John Vanbrugh designed the building and lived there between 1717 and 1726. The castle was known as 'The Bastille' both because of its appearance — resembling a medieval fortress — and because its architect had been held in the French prison as an English spy.

through the middle of his building. This effectively made the Queen's House the centrepiece of his design, a role the building is simply not grand enough to fulfil.

Next to the Naval College is the Trafalgar Tavern ❿ on Park Row. It was built in 1837 and became famous for its Cabinet Whitebait Dinners when members of the Government would come down the Thames in barges to dine there. The pub is mentioned in Charles Dickens' *Our Mutual Friend* and the author was a regular visitor.

Down the alleyway behind the Trafalgar is Trinity Hospital ❿. It was established in 1613 by the Earl of Norfolk who founded a number of such charitable institutions. Today it still fulfils its original purpose of providing homes for the

▶*Trafalgar Tavern, on the Thames, dates from 1837 and was visited regularly by Charles Dickens.*

THE SOUTH EAST

DAVID SELLMAN

Clumps of pearly grey sea-holly and pink roses grow on the dunes, along with sea sandwort, ragwort and the common mallow. Lady's bedstraw and wild asparagus border the paths, and bulrushes, reeds and the giant sharp rush grow in the water margins.

The dunes are also the location of the Royal St George's golf club, whose famous links course **A**, the venue for several Open Championships, is crossed by the walk.

You return to the town to walk

◀ *Willow Cottage, with its smart, bright paintwork, is part of a jettied, timber-framed row in Church Street.*

Three walks in one around an ancient Cinque Port

In the Middle Ages, the town of Sandwich was one of England's most flourishing ports. One of the original Cinque Ports, it stood at the southern end of the Wantsum, the navigable channel that separated the Isle of Thanet from the mainland.

In the 15th century, the Wantsum silted up and Sandwich lost its sea harbour. The town's importance faded, but this has helped to preserve its fabric. Today, it is one of the most complete medieval towns in the country.

This walk has three distinct parts. The first takes you from Sandwich to the sea and back across a famous golf course; the second takes you out to see the remains of Roman Richborough Castle, which guarded the entrance to the Wantsum; and the third explores the town itself.

The walk begins at The Quay; the Butts Stream and the Delf River thread their ways through the town and the quays on the Stour give an impression of how lively the medieval port once was.

WILDLIFE HABITAT

In its 400-year retreat from Sandwich, the sea left salt marshes, sand dunes and tidal mud-flats in its wake. The walk heads across this new land, which provides important wildlife habitats. Redshanks, shelduck, ringed plovers and little terns breed here. Sanderlings, grey plovers, snow buntings and hen harriers can be found in the winter, and Sandwich Bay is a stopping off place for many migrant birds.

ANDREW CLEAVE/NATURE PHOTOGRAPHERS

◀ *Giant sharp rush grows on the sand dunes at Royal St George's golf links; this is one of its few English sites.*

FACT FILE

☀	Sandwich, 12 miles (19.2km) east of Canterbury, on the A257
OS	Pathfinders 1212 (TR 25/35) and 1196 (TR 26/36), grid reference TR 332582

miles 0 1 2 3 4 5 6 7 8 9 10 miles
kms 0 1 2 3 4 5 6 7 8 9 10 11 12 13 14 15 kms

◔	Allow at least 4 hours
▬	Level walking on good paths and pavements
P	On the quay at the start
T	B R Sandwich. For details of services run by East Kent Buses, Tel. (01304) 240024. River bus to Richborough, Tel. (01304) 820171
¶	A wide range of pubs, cafés and restaurants in Sandwich
⌂	Richborough Castle (English Heritage) open April-Oct, Tel. (01304) 612013. Precinct Toy Collection open Easter-Sept, Mon-Sat 10.30am-4.30pm, Sun 2-4.30pm; Oct, Sat-Sun 2-4.30pm (admission charge). Guildhall and Museum, Tel. (01304) 617197. White Hill Folk Museum, Tel. (01304) 612076
I	Tourist Info. at Guildhall May-Sept, Tel. (01304) 613565; winter, Tel. (01304) 369576

THE WALK

SANDWICH

The walk begins on The Quay.

▶ 1 Walk down the tree-lined avenue, with the River Stour on your left. At the end, turn left over a footbridge, then right. After 10 paces, follow the right-hand one of two concrete footpath markers along the tarmac path. Bear right at the fork, following yellow waymarks. Follow the path towards the sea, along a dyke known as Green Wall to a footbridge over The New Cut. Cross and bear half-right uphill towards the dunes. Cross a minor road and go through the kissing-gate onto the golf course **A**. Follow the clearly marked route to the sea.

▶ 2 Turn left along the shoreline, towards the burnt-out clubhouse. At a gate, follow footpath markers, keeping close to the golf course fence on your left. Turn left with the fence and follow a well worn cart track towards the church tower on the horizon ahead, passing two derelict houses and an alder plantation on your right. Cross a stile and turn left onto a road. After 20 paces, turn right beside an electricity sub-station. Climb up to the gates and cross The New Cut.

◀ *Upper Strand Street would have thronged with people when Sandwich was England's leading commercial port.*

The ramparts rise above the ditches to a height of 20 feet (6m), in places forming an angle of 60°. The best place for seeing the mighty chimneys of The Salutation, which was designed by Sir Edwin Lutyens in 1911, is from The Bulwarks at the start of the wall-top walk.

At the other end of the wall, between the Stour and a road, is Gazen Salts Nature Reserve **C**, one of three reserves in the area. You continue past it and head north for 1½ miles (2.4km), to Richborough **D**.

This stretch of coast has for thousands of years been the landfall for invaders of all kinds; birds, butterflies, windborne seeds and armies.

In AD43, the Romans established a bridgehead at Richborough, which they called Rutupiae. Initially, it was a supply base, but by the end of the century an enormous triumphal arch stood on the promontory facing the sea, making it eminently clear that Imperial Rome ruled here.

ARCH ENEMIES

A settlement grew around the arch, but by the second century barbarian invaders were making life in Britain less secure. The arch was demolished, leaving only the base, which can still be seen. A fort covering 5 acres (2 hectares) was built; its walls still stand to a height of 25 feet (7.5m), striking testimony to the potential gravity of the Anglo-Saxon raids (see box).

You return to Sandwich the way

around the massive ramparts of its 14th-century walls **B**, which line the town's landward side. They might have been designed for the 20th-century tourist; from their heights, you can see the closely grouped roofs of the town dominated by the three remaining church towers.

Follow the embankment path beside the River Stour to the footbridge you crossed earlier. Retrace your earlier steps to the playground on your left. Climb the bank onto the Old Town Wall/Bulwarks path, and walk towards a bridge.

■3 At the end of the Bulwarks, cross the Sandown road and continue on Mill Wall. Cross New Street onto Rope Walk. At Moat Sole, cross and walk along the Butts **B** to the Canterbury Road. Cross to the information board at Gallows Field.

■4 If you wish to visit Gazen Salts Nature Reserve **C**, follow the signs. Otherwise, turn left and follow the railings round to your right, into Richborough Road. Continue for ½ mile (800m). Just beyond the scrapyard on your right, turn off at the footpath marker for the Saxon Shore Way and the Stour Valley Walk. Go under the viaduct and continue, to a stile and cast-iron gate at the railway.

■5 Cross the railway line and another stile. Turn right along the road. After 250 yards (220m), turn right up the private road signposted for Richborough Castle **D**. Follow the footpath past the fort entrance, then alongside the fort, high above the river. The path drops downhill to the railway. Cross a stile, the railway line and another stile, then turn sharp right between the river and the railway. Cross a sluice gate and return to point 5. Retrace your steps to the Gallows Field information board. Continue ahead along Strand Street **E**, past St Mary's Church **F** to The Precinct, and the Toy Museum **G** at the bottom of Harnet Street.

■6 Walk along Harnet Street to the Guildhall **H**. Cross the old Cattle Market to the start of New Street. Turn left towards the Delf Street and Market Street signboards, then right into King Street. You pass St Peter's **J**. Just beyond the post office, turn left into Short Street. Go right along the High Street, then left into Church Street to St Clement's **K**. Retrace your steps and turn right along Fisher Street. Walk along Fisher Street into Quay Lane, and past Fisher Gate **L** to return to the start of the walk.

▲As you return to Sandwich from the seaside, the path leads alongside Sandwich Haven. A little further on, ducks can be seen enjoying the sheltered waters of the Butts Stream (below).

ALL PHOTOS: DAVID SELLMAN

you came. To wander anywhere in the town is a delight, and the route can only cover the principal sights. Strand Street **E**, the old harbourside street, is full of timber-framed houses, many disguised by later brick fronts. Manwood Court, with its crow-stepped gables, was built as a grammar school in 1580 in Sandwich brick. Made from the local river mud, this brick can be seen all over the town.

At the corner of Paradise Row, a decorated stone doorway in a wall is all that remains of a prosperous early 14th-century house.

The jettied Long House is 16th-century, with an 18th-century false front that is best seen from the east end. The name of nearby Monken Quay recalls the presence of its owners in the Middle Ages, the monks of Christchurch, Canterbury.

SAD AND EMPTY

At the junction with Church Street is the King's Arms, which has a corner bracket, dated 1592, carved as a satyr. Opposite the pub is St Mary's Church **F**, a sad relic of town decay. The central tower fell in 1668, irretrievably damaging the early 12th-century interior. Now redundant,

▶The Old House on Strand Street provided rooms for pilgrims making their way to Canterbury Cathedral.

the barn-like church has a desolate feel to it inside.

Beyond St Mary's is the Old House. Once a hostel for pilgrims on their way to Canterbury, this, too, is a timber-framed building refaced in

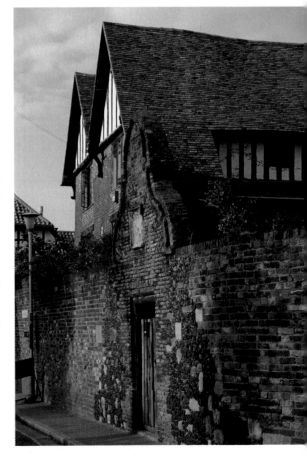

brick, in 1713.

The Toy Museum **G**, of interest to all ages, faces you across The Precinct, while in Harnet Street is a Georgian milestone inscribed with the distances to Deal, Canterbury and London. Close by is a blocked, 15th-century wooden doorway with roses in the spandrels. In the fine-coursed flint wall opposite can be seen the remains of a Gothic arch.

At the top of Harnet Street, you turn left to the Guildhall **H**, whose showpiece is a 17th-century court-room with a collapsible jury box. The floor could be cleared to leave it free for the merchants of the various guilds to trade. In the council cham-ber above is the mayor's chair, which dates from 1561.

▲The milestone in Harnet Street dates from the 18th century. Close by is the Guildhall (below) with a fine coat of arms above its doors.

Roman Forts of the Saxon Shore

Richborough Castle, the walk's northern objective, was built by the Romans.

Roman Britain was in the forefront of the struggle to repel the barbarian invasions that beset the empire in the second century. Saxon pirates from northern Germany attacked shipping along the east coast. The Thames, the Wash and the Humber gave access to river systems penetrating the whole of central Britain, and these had to be protected from invaders.

The Roman fleet was based at Portus Lemanis and Dover. Rochester, Caister-on-Sea (near Great Yarmouth) and Brough (on the Humber) were also used. In the early third century, masonry forts were built at Reculver and Brancaster. Brough on Humber was

strengthened. The Richborough monument was made into a lookout post, and by AD290 was replaced by the present Saxon Shore fort.

After the death of Constantine in AD337, raids increased. Defences were reorganized, by order of a Count of the Saxon Shore. Pevensey was the last major addition to the Saxon Shore forts. In AD367, the barbarians invaded from all sides. Hadrian's Wall fell and the Count of the Saxon Shore was killed. In AD410, the Emperor Honorius instructed the British to look to their own defences as he could do no more for them.

The old cattle market around the Guildhall has become a car park. Beyond it, narrow streets cluster round St Peter's **J**, another victim of the town's inability to repair its buildings. The central tower fell in 1661, removing the south aisle. The townsfolk could only afford to rebuild in Sandwich brick.

ANGEL ROOF

The present parish church, St Clement's **K**, still has its Norman crossing tower, with three tiers of arcading outside and another inside. The angel roof is more typical of East Anglian churches, but the style spread south as a result of the strong maritime links between the Cinque Ports and Great Yarmouth during the Middle Ages.

From St Clement's, you make for Fisher Street, a fine example of the variety of buildings in Sandwich. Jetties, Georgian and Victorian red-bricks and walls washed green, pink, cream and grey stand side by side. A Victorian gas lamp on a bracket is still operational.

From here, Quay Lane leads to Fisher Gate **L**. Built in 1384 after the French first sacked the town, it is the only remaining town gate, and is built in faced flints up to the string course. Above that, it was restored by the Cooper's Guild in 1560 in Sandwich brick. It is interesting to compare the black-brick diaper pat-tern as seen from Quay Lane with the pattern on the seaward side, where workmen got it wrong!

RAY GRANGER

Exploring the architectural delights of a flamboyant resort

FACT FILE

※ Brighton, East Sussex

⌖ Pathfinder 1307 (TQ 20/30), grid reference TQ 310048. A street plan, such as the OS 1: 10,000 map, is most useful

miles 0 1 2 3 4 5 6 7 8 9 10 miles
kms 0 1 2 3 4 5 6 7 8 9 10 11 12 13 14 15 kms

◖ Allow 4 hours to include visits

▬ A town walk along made-up roads; a few hills

P Car parks at station and elsewhere. Avoid on-street voucher system

T Regular trains, buses and coaches

⊞ Many pubs, restaurants and cafés in Brighton

WC At the station, the seafront and Pavilion Gardens (off North Street)

⌂ The Royal Pavilion: Tel. (01273) 603005

▲The Royal Pavilion has undergone many changes in its 200-year history but is instantly recognizable. The bottlenose dolphin (below) is seen occasionally from Brighton's beach.

NHPA

Until the mid-18th century, Brighton was a simple fishing and farming village. It was just a cluster of houses by the pebble beach, surrounded by common fields — known locally as laines — which extended up into the down-land. Dr Richard Russell, from the nearby county town of Lewes, changed all that. A passionate believer in the curative powers of seawater, he began recommending Brighton's bathing beach as a cure for all ills. As a result, from about 1750, 'Doctor Brighton' became a resort for the rich and fashionable.

HOME FROM HOME

After a visit in 1783, George, Prince of Wales, decided to make Brighton his seaside home. The town became a marine extension of London society, inspiring a frenzy of speculative building, some of it on a very grand scale, that lasted over 40 years.

The Prince, later Prince Regent, then George IV, retained his affection for Brighton throughout his life, but when he died in 1830 fashionable interest in the town died with him. The opening of the railway in 1841 ensured that the visitors kept coming and the town kept growing, but the glory days were over.

By the mid-20th century, Brighton

THE WALK

BRIGHTON – HOVE

The route starts from Brighton BR station.

1 After admiring the station **A**, leave by the main exit and walk down the left-hand side of Queen's Road ahead. Take the next left (a steep path leading into Gloucester Road) and walk downhill into the grid of streets known as the North Laine. Follow the road down until you reach a pedestrian area surrounded by curio shops, and turn right into narrow, cobbled Kensington Gardens. At the end turn right and then left along Gardner Street, emerging on Church Street.

2 Turn left here and walk downhill, towards the outbuildings of the Royal Pavilion **B**. Cross the road and walk on, past the entrances to the Corn Exchange, the Dome and the museum, glancing inside if possible. Keep going past the imposing North

Gateway belonging to the pavilion estate, and follow the pavement of the Old Steine **C** as it curves around the east front of the Royal Pavilion.

3 At the end of the pavilion lawn, turn left up to Palace Place, which leads out onto North Street. Turn right, cross the busy street at the lights and keep going uphill until you reach Meeting House Lane, a narrow alleyway indicated by a sign that directs you left into the maze of streets and 'twittens' known as The Lanes **D**.

4 Follow the lane to a green shop front where it turns sharp left, then right again. Take the next left, between two antique jewellery shops, to emerge in Market Street — a triangular area that was originally the market place of the old town. Turn right, past the front of The Pump House, and right again along Nile Street, past the brand-new, neoclassical Nile House. At the end of Nile Street bear right up Prince Albert Street, cross over the road and turn left down Ship Street to come to the seafront.

5 Turn left and cross the busy seafront road by a pedestrian crossing, then turn right along the seafront, past the Brighton Centre and the adjacent Grand Hotel **E**, towards the derelict West Pier **F**. Opposite the Grand Hotel, turn left down the steps to the lower esplanade to escape the traffic, but keep walking westward, past the bandstand. Continue along the beach to the broad esplanade of Hove Sea Wall, noticing the spectacular Regency

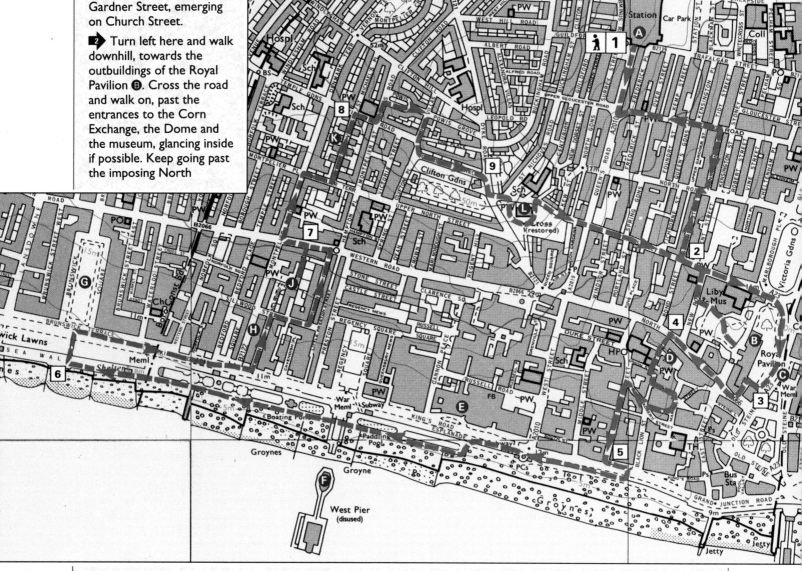

West Pier (disused)

development of Brunswick Terrace and Brunswick Square on your right.

6 Take the path across the lawn towards Brunswick Square **G** for a closer look, then turn back along the seafront road. Just past the bandstand, turn up Oriental Place **H**. At the end, turn right then left up Sillwood Road to Western Road. Turn left, then left again down Western Terrace to see

the Western Pavilion **J**.

7 On emerging from Western Terrace, cross Western Road and walk left towards the crossroads. Turn right up Montpelier Road. At a road junction turn right, then left up Montpelier Villas **K**.

8 At the next junction, turn right and then left around St Michael's Church. Turn right into Powis Square. Leave it by

the road at the far side and turn right at the next junction, walking downhill and bearing to the left along the raised pavement that runs along the edge of Clifton Terrace.

9 At the end of Clifton Terrace cross the main road, then turn right and shortly left into Church Street. Cross into the churchyard of St Nicholas's **L**, with its intriguing monuments. Take the path

to the right of the church, turn right onto Church Street and follow it downhill to the junction with busy Queen's Road. Cross over and carry on down Church Street. Just before you reach the Corn Exchange turn right along New Road, then left to the Pavilion Gardens and the palace entrance. Retrace your steps up Gardner Street, off Church Street, to the start of the walk.

---

had declined into a somewhat down-at-heel resort with a shady reputation — inspiring Graham Greene to write *Brighton Rock* — but nonetheless it remains unique. No other town can offer its heady mixture of faded elegance, outright fantasy and good-humoured sleaze.

The walk starts in Brighton Station **A**, once the terminus of the London, Brighton & South Coast Railway, which has an elegant curved canopy of iron and glass. Look for the dolphin design, the emblem of Brighton, on the spandrels between the main arches.

From the station you dive straight into backstreet Brighton as you enter

▲*The brightly painted cast iron and wrought iron of the station roof are in keeping with this lively resort.*

the North Laine area. Originally, this was an open field divided into strips of ploughland grouped into furlongs; the broad streets running downhill follow the routes of old trackways between each furlong, while the narrow cross-streets, such as Kensington Gardens, are built along the strips. The area is now full of interesting small shops.

To the south lie the outbuildings of the Royal Pavilion **B**. In the 1930s, the Prince's magnificent stables and indoor riding hall were converted into the Dome concert hall and the Corn Exchange. A later range of stables had already been transformed into a town museum

◄*The Corn Exchange, on Church Street, was built as an indoor riding school for the Prince Regent. The gardens of the Old Steine (right), in front of the Royal Pavilion, are flanked by large houses.*

and library. The museum, in particular, is well worth a visit.

As you walk around the front of the pavilion, notice the many fine town houses on the Old Steine **C**. These were built to accommodate the prince's courtiers and his mistress, Maria Fitzherbert.

THROUGH THE TWITTENS

When it was built, the Royal Pavilion was on the very edge of the old town, the area now known as The Lanes **D**. Bounded by East Street, North Street and West Street, this area is riddled with narrow 'twittens' — alleyways that thread their way between buildings that date back to the 16th century. Many are occupied by antique dealers, but an exception is The Pump House, a timber-built pub with an early 19th-century facade clad in black 'mathematical tiles' — a form of hanging tile carefully designed to resemble glazed brickwork. Almost nothing remains of the medieval

village, much of it having been swallowed up by the sea.

On the seafront is the Grand Hotel **E**, whose centre was blown out by a terrorist bomb in October 1984. The hotel has now been rebuilt and enlarged. The decaying West Pier **F** is widely regarded as the finest of all Victorian piers, but seems likely to fall into the sea unless the West Pier Trust can raise sufficient funds to restore it. Much of it has already vanished, unable to withstand the high sea winds over the last 20 years.

REGENCY TERRACES

Just down the seafront, past Hove bandstand, is a more durable monument to past glories. Brunswick Terrace and Brunswick Square **G** are the heart of Brunswick Town, a speculative development built on open farmland between 1824 and 1828. Inspired by the Nash terraces of Regent's Park, the scheme was the work of local architects Amon Wilds and Charles Busby, although the massive neoclassical facades and bow fronts are more Busby's style than his partner's. Along with Wilds' son Amon Henry, they designed many of the finest housing schemes in Regency Brighton.

One of these is Oriental Place **H**, which bears the unmistakable trademark of Amon Henry Wilds. Completed in 1827, the terraces are adorned with classical pillars whose capitals are carved in the shape of ammonites — the architect chose this pun on his name as his motif.

The young Wilds let his imagination run riot in this area and built a

BRIGHTON BOROUGH COUNCIL

▲*An IRA bomb at the Grand Hotel, where Mrs Thatcher and the cabinet were staying, terminated the 1984 Conservative Party Conference.*

host of houses in various styles (many now demolished), culminating in the Western Pavilion **J**, a miniature version of the Royal Pavilion, which was his home for several years from 1833. The Gothic House opposite, designed in 1822 by his father, exploited the 19th-century craze for Gothic ruins.

PRIVATE'S SECRET

Montpelier Villas **K**, designed in 1845, towards the end of Amon Henry Wilds's career, is arguably his finest work. The bold eaves and projecting, canopied bow windows are typical of his later work, though his motif is absent.

St Nicholas's Church **L** is Brighton's original parish church and the only medieval building surviving in the town. Near the door is the grave of one Phoebe Hessel, who died in 1821 after serving for several years as a private soldier in the 5th Regiment of Foot — an eccentricity typical of Brighton.

The Royal Pavilion

Brighton's Royal Pavilion is probably the most extravagant, astonishing and entertaining palace in northern Europe. A sparkling cocktail of Chinese, Indian and Gothic styles, gathered together with a total disregard for authenticity, scale or common sense, it is a fitting monument to the profligate prince who was its inspiration

George, Prince of Wales, was an avid follower of architectural fashion. Within a year of acquiring the lease of the airy but modest Brighton House, in 1786, he instructed his architect, Henry Holland, to transform it into something more befitting his station — a 'marine pavilion' over twice the size of the original house, with a domed rotunda and a colonnade.

Not content, he ordered a new portico and conservatory, and engaged William Porden to build a new stable block in the garden. Porden's response was a spectacular Indian-style roundhouse that is now the Dome concert hall. The prince was enchanted. Wryly observing that his horses were better housed than he was, he immediately started

DAVE JACOBS/ROBERT HARDING PICTURE LIBRARY

The present Royal Pavilion has been extensively restored after damage by fire.

planning a complete revamp of the pavilion, ultimately engaging John Nash to turn his dreams into reality. Nash made the most of his opportunity, whisking brick, stucco and cast iron into a flamboyant confection of pinnacles, minarets and onion domes. The interior is, if anything, even more astounding. Glittering with gold leaf and glowing with colour, it is a delight to visit.

▼*Brighton sprang from the fishing hamlet of Brighthelmstone but is now home to numerous leisure craft.*

RAY GRANGER

Walking up through a green valley to lovely Dorset heathland

The low cliffs on the coast at Bournemouth are cut occasionally by valleys known as 'chines'. Bournemouth's first houses were built on either side of the main chine, where the River Bourne flowed from watermeadows over golden sand into the sea. This walk follows the Bourne through the town and then over heathland to a 19th-century model village.

The Bourne's 'mouth' is now in a pipe, though at low tide the water can still be seen running into the sea just east of the Pier, where the walk begins. The valley's meadows, where boats were once washed up

MIKE READ/SWIFT PICTURE LIBRARY

FACT FILE

⁎ Bournemouth

▯▭ Pathfinder 1301 (SU 00/SZ 09), grid reference SZ 088907

miles 0 1 2 3 4 5 6 7 8 9 10 miles
kms 0 1 2 3 4 5 6 7 8 9 10 11 12 13 14 15 kms

◑ Allow 2 hours

▭ Two short, steep climbs on the heath. Can be boggy by the stream

P Car park to east of pier or elsewhere in town

T BR station 1 mile (1.6km) from the start. Bournemouth is well served by buses and coaches

🍴 A wide variety of pubs, cafés and restaurants in Bournemouth; King's Arms, Talbot Village

▲ The town rises up beyond the beach where the River Bourne meets the sea. The lowland heath of Dorset is home to the smooth snake (left), one of Britain's rarest animals, now protected by law.

LEIGH HATTS

at very high tides, are now the Lower Pleasure Gardens **Ⓐ**, with the stream serving as a natural paddling pool as it passes the bandstand.

The seaside town of Bournemouth began in 1810, when one Louis Tregonwell built a house on the side of the valley. As a customs official, Tregonwell had patrolled the beach for smugglers, and enjoyed the location. The house survives in Exeter Road as the enlarged Royal Exeter Hotel, earning its royal status when the Empress of Austria stayed there in 1888.

Nearby is the massive Bournemouth International Conference Centre, built on the site of a thatched cottage where Charles Darwin stayed in 1862 while looking for flowers by the brook. The heroine of

Hardy's *Tess of the d'Urbervilles* 'lived' across the valley in Westover Road, for this is his 'Sandbourne'.

Looking down on the Upper Pleasure Gardens is the massive town hall **Ⓑ**. Set back here is the tower of the late 19th-century St Stephen's Church, which was described by the poet John Betjeman as 'the best church in Bournemouth'.

CASTELLATED TOWER

Further on, through the tranquil valley, you pass a red-brick, castellated tower hiding in the foliage. There is a marked change when the valley opens out and enters the Borough of Poole. Here, weeping willows have been planted by the water and two streams join to form the Bourne. The one from the north comes via a short underground channel from the Coy Pond **Ⓒ**. The pond, never a real 'decoy' for entrapping wildfowl, was created in 1886 when the northern stream was piped under a new railway embankment.

flyover to the River Bourne. Follow the stream through the Lower Pleasure Gardens **A** to The Square. At the final bridge, go right through a tunnel, and then bear left in front of WH Smith's.

▶2 Cross two roads into the Upper Pleasure Gardens, and pass the war memorial and town hall **B**. Under the high flyover, cross the stream to continue on the other bank. Go straight over Queens Road and down steps on the right to follow

of Wales Road into the longest section of valley. A path leads down to the grass and stream. At the next bridge, cross and follow a trodden footpath along the other bank.

▶3 Cross Branksome Wood Road to enter the final section of Gardens. Go over the first footbridge and up the steps opposite to cross a road by Coy Pond **C**.

▶4 Keep to the right of the pond on a path that curves round the feeder

stream. Go up the few steps behind and turn right along a road. At the far end, a flight of steps leads up to a footpath. At a road, turn left to cross the railway and reach Talbot Heath **D**.

▶5 Bear half right on a narrow footpath, onto the open heathland. Where the path divides at the top and bottom of the hill, keep to the left. The path runs towards a wire fence and the northern branch of the Bourne.

▶6 Do not cross the footbridge, but go right between tall poles. At a junction, turn left along an enclosed path between fields. The path later runs through a belt of pine trees. After a short distance, go up a steep slope and bear right. Ahead is Talbot Village's church tower **E**. At a T-junction of paths, turn left. Turn right into Talbot Drive. At the far end go left to a crossing by a pub, then double back along the far side of the road into Talbot Village. By the church is the bus stop for the service back into Bournemouth.

BOURNEMOUTH – TALBOT VILLAGE

This linear walk begins at Bournemouth Pier. A bus service operates from the far end of the route back to where the walk began.

▶1 Go inland under the

the waterside. At a waterfall, cross to the other side to pass a tall, castellated folly. As the path swings away, keep ahead over the grass to reach some steps on the right at the end of this section. Cross over Prince

---

▼*This castellated folly hides between trees and shrubbery in Bournemouth's peaceful Upper Pleasure Gardens.*

The stream feeding the pond comes from Canford Heath via Bourne Bottom, below Talbot Heath **D**. This isolated segment of Dorset heathland, 160 feet (48m) above the end of the valley, is arguably among the finest in western Europe.

RARE SPECIES

The purple heather once made bee-keeping common, and the heath hosts many rare or endangered species such as the smooth snake and the sand lizard. The nightjar and hobby are among the rare birds that may be seen here, along with the elusive Dartford warbler.

As you approach Talbot Village, a 75-foot (22.5-m) church tower **E** is

the only clue that within the large pinewood beyond Talbot Heath lies a secret model village. It was planned in 1850 by philanthropist Georgina Talbot, who was inspired to help the poor after reading a German book, *The Goldiggers Village*.

Each cottage was set in an acre (4,047 square metres) of land, and had a well and a pigsty. There is also a school and Gothic almshouses, built of Portland stone. Each villager promised to 'Love God, keep the Commandments and honour the Queen'. The church, which was completed in 1870, had clockwork chimes; Georgina Talbot feared that if bell ringers were employed they might spend their fees on drink.

architectural delights of one of the finest small towns in England. The broad street called The Plains opens to the left, bounded on one side by carefully converted warehouses and on the other by elegantly restored Georgian buildings.

The openness of The Plains is in sharp contrast to narrow Fore Street, which rises steeply through the heart of the town. The small shops lining this street are discreetly built

◀ *The car park where the walk starts overlooks the waters at Steamer Quay, which provide moorings for pleasure boats. The buff ermine moth (inset) thrives on the damp conditions hereabouts. This fine Gothic building off Fore Street (below), complete with battlements, is used as an art gallery.*

FACT FILE

- Totnes, 5 miles (8km) west of Torbay, on the A385

- Outdoor Leisure Map 20 and Pathfinder 1341 (SX 76/77), grid reference SX 806599

  miles 0 1 2 3 4 5 6 7 8 9 10 miles
  kms 0 1 2 3 4 5 6 7 8 9 10 11 12 13 14 15 kms

- Allow at least 2½ hours

- The town section includes a steep climb up Fore Street, and a long climb up Harper's Hill; Coplands Lane is very wet and muddy after rain

- P Long-stay car park at the start (fee payable)

- T Totnes is on the main London-Plymouth BR line. Buses from most South Devon towns. Regular boat services from Dartmouth

- Several pubs, restaurants, cafés and tea-rooms in Totnes

- WC At start; three others in town

- I For tourist information, including details of Totnes Castle, Tel. (01803) 863168

Architectural delights and old lanes in a period-piece town

Totnes can surprise the visitor from the start. This is the lowest crossing point of the tidal River Dart, but it is not particularly wide, and does not look very deep. Yet high water brings ocean-going ships upriver to the town's doorstep. Opposite Steamer Quay, where the walk begins, large freighters can be seen unloading cargoes of timber. This is not an industrial scene, though; no docks blight the waterfront, and the commercial activity blends easily with the leisure craft and passenger cruisers that ply regularly between Totnes and Dartmouth.

MOTOR MUSEUM

Further up Steamer Quay is Totnes Motor Museum ❶, where vintage, sports and racing cars of famous international marques form the backbone of an exhibition covering eight decades of motoring.

Crossing Totnes Bridge brings you the first glimpse of the many

into the frontages of the old buildings. A timbered top storey overhangs the bottom one; and it is always worthwhile looking up at the top storeys to see intriguing architectural details.

The arch of the East Gate ❷, the town's best known landmark, straddles the street near the top of the rise. This medieval gateway was almost lost in 1990 when fire, traditionally a scourge in Totnes's close-packed streets, caused serious damage. The gateway has now been

THE WALK

TOTNES

The walk begins at the car park at Steamer Quay.

▶ **1** With the river on your left, follow the quayside, then turn left along Steamer Quay Road. Pass the motor museum **A** and turn left at the T-junction.

▶ **2** At the next T-junction, turn left and cross Totnes Bridge. At the mini-roundabout, go to the left of the Royal Seven Stars Hotel. Walk up Fore Street to the East Gate **B**.

▶ **3** Turn right into Guildhall Yard, directly under the arch, climbing two flights of stone steps. Turn left into the churchyard of St Mary's **C**. Follow the path around the church to the opposite side, passing one gate and turning left through the next, to emerge in front of the guildhall **D**.

▶ **4** Turn left out of the church gate and left again into a narrow alley. Turn right into the High Street ahead. Follow the road as it narrows and curves left. Where the main route swings right, keep straight ahead (with the Bull Inn on your left) to the junction with the main road (Totnes Bypass) at the top.

▶ **5** Cross to the lane opposite, marked 'Harper's Hill Unsuitable for Motors', and follow it to a junction at the top of the hill.

▶ **6** Turn right. After ½ mile (800m), turn right down the unmarked track that drops away in front of a small clump of trees that form a high hedge. Fork right near the bottom.

Continue to a crossroads. Go ahead on the road opposite, and cross the railway bridge. The road rises.

▶ **7** At the top, turn right through a break in the hedgerow along a muddy, overgrown green lane. Continue for about ¾ mile (1.2km) to a junction with a new road and housing development (not shown on the map). Bear right to another junction, then turn right. Continue to a T-junction with a main road.

▶ **8** Cross, bear left and turn almost immediately right into Malt Mill. Go under the railway bridge and turn left. Keep on the right of the road. With The Globe pub on your left, bear right into Castle Street.

▶ **9** After a few paces, turn sharp right up a narrow tarmac path between high walls. Keep ahead into Castle Street. Go under a stone arch, then turn sharp right up a tiny rising path to Totnes Castle **E**. Return to Castle Street and continue to a T-junction. Turn left into the High Street and retrace your steps across the bridge to the start.

(sideways) MIKE WILLIAMS

fully restored, at vast expense.

Just off Fore Street, beyond the East Gate, is the Church of St Mary **C**. Its unusually red sandstone is almost incandescent on a bright day. The stone rood screen inside is one of the finest in Britain.

◀ *A view over the skyline of Totnes to the squat, circular castle keep.*

Beside the church stands the guildhall **D**, on the site of the refectory of an 11th-century Benedictine priory dedicated to St Mary. The town's mayors have been chosen here for over 400 years.

QUIET LANES

As you head away from the centre, the narrow street closes in still further. A bypass marks the boundary of the built-up area; crossing it marks a sudden break. Only a few strides into Harper's Hill, the hubbub fades to silence. The tarmac lane gives way to a broken, stony track, which rises relentlessly for ½ mile (800m) over Windmill Down. Until the mid-18th century, this lonely green lane was the Plymouth road.

From the top of the hill, Dartmoor fills the horizon to the distant north and west. Here and there, where the arable land has been freshly broken, patches of rich red earth show through against the green.

The return to town is along another old lane. Copland Lane is often wet and overgrown; clumps of great plantain cover the ground around pools of standing water.

Totnes Castle **E** lies at the end of the walk's circuit. The 15-foot-thick (4.5-m) walls of its circular keep are remarkably intact, largely because no serious battles took place here. As a viewpoint over the town and the surrounding area, though, the castle is as dominant as it ever was. It is open to the public during the summer and there is no better place from which to survey Totnes before returning to the start.

Hall, passing the House of Correction or the Old County Gaol. This lane leads to the castle Ⓐ.

This was the last fortification built at Montgomery. It was preceded by a hill fort, visited later on the walk, the Roman Forden Gaer and a Norman motte and bailey at Hen Domen, both situated to the north of the town. All four were built to control the main route into mid Wales. The border hills, which at that time were covered in forest, presented an obstacle for any army — but the

◄ *The commanding view from the castle serves as a reminder of its once-important role in the defence of Wales. Found on old walls, ivy-leaved toadflax (inset) flowers from May to September.*

JEREMY MOORE. INSET: M I GARWOOD/NHPA

FACT FILE

✳ Montgomery, 17 miles (27.2km) north-west of Ludlow

▭ Pathfinder 909 (SO 29/39), grid reference SO 222964

miles 0 1 2 3 4 5 6 7 8 9 10 miles
kms 0 1 2 3 4 5 6 7 8 9 10 11 12 13 14 15 kms

◔ Allow 2 hours

▬ Footpaths, roads and pavements. One steady climb. Boots advisable in wet weather

P In Broad Street or the town centre

🍴 Pubs and restaurants in town

wc Behind the Town Hall

largely halted at that point; nearby Newtown and Welshpool were much better sited for canal and then rail services. Montgomery remains largely Georgian, and the whole town is a conservation area, with an active Civic Society whose role is to preserve its character.

This walk encompasses the town, its castle, and the hills to the west, which give fine views over Shropshire and to the mountains of mid Wales. You start in Broad Street and climb the hill behind the Town

A ruined castle and a well-preserved Georgian county town

Montgomery has been of strategic importance since at least the Iron Age. Roman and Norman military commanders also recognized its potential importance, and it remained a significant point to control during the Civil War. After peace was restored, its defences became obsolete, but it continued to prosper as a county town into Georgian times.

Its further development was

▶ *A steady climb takes you to the top of Town Hill where a war memorial stands, recalling both World Wars.*

JEREMY MOORE

THE WALK

MONTGOMERY – FFRIDD FALDWYN

The walk starts from Broad Street in the town centre.

1 Take the road to the left of the Town Hall and climb up the hill past the Dragon Hotel and the House of Correction to the castle car park on the right. Go through the car park and take the footpath on the left along the ridge to the castle ruins **A**. Return to the car park.

2 Cross the road at the car park entrance to a footpath through a kissing-gate. This path soon meets a sunken lane that follows the line of the Town Ditch. Continue up the lane as the ditch bears off to the left. The lane climbs up to the top of the ridge, through some Scots pines, and on to the memorial at the summit of Town Hill **B**. Retrace your steps along the lane, past the footpath off to the right which you came up, to the road.

3 Turn left up the road, past the town reservoir. Where the road begins to descend, just before two road signs ('Steep Hill' and 'Bends'), cross a stile to the right into a field. Climb the bank opposite and cross a wooden fence to Ffridd Faldwyn **C**. Follow the grassy path going straight over the hill and down through Baldwyn's Wood, swinging right to meet the B4385 underneath the castle rock.

4 Turn right along the road. After passing a left turn to Welshpool, take the next left into Gaol Road towards the imposing front of the County Gaol **D**. Before reaching it, turn right immediately after a short stone wall. This leads through the end of a modern housing development to Chirbury Road. Turn right past the Bricklayer's Arms towards a T-junction. Just before you reach the junction, turn left into a narrow road called School Bank. At the top, turn right into Church Bank. Keeping alongside the church **E** on your right, follow the road round the churchyard to descend into Broad Street.

River Severn cuts through this obstruction and deep into the Welsh heartland, and could be forded here.

The medieval stone castle, on its commanding rocky outcrop, was built between 1223 and 1225. It was besieged by the Welsh on more than one occasion but did not fall. Its end came in 1649. It had been a Royalist stronghold during the Civil War, and the victorious Parliament ordered its destruction.

You now retrace your steps to climb the local viewpoint of Town Hill **B**. The route crosses the remains of the Town Ditch, part of the castle fortifications which encompassed the town. At the summit of Town Hill is a war memorial and a panoramic view indicator. To the east and south are The Long Mynd, the Stiperstones and Corndon Hill, and to the west Kerry Hill, Cadair Idris and Aran Fawddwy are visible on a clear day.

ANCIENT ORIGINS

From here, you walk to the hill fort of Ffridd Faldwyn **C**. The impressive earthworks date from the late Iron Age, but within these are the remains of an earlier habitation from Neolithic times. The descent back into the town is made through Baldwyn's Wood. Baldwin de Boulers was the Norman lord during the time of Henry I, and the Welsh name for the town, Trefaldwyn, derives from his name. The English name comes from Roger Montgomery, the Norman earl responsible for building the motte and bailey castle at Hen Domen.

IMPOSING GAOL

Back in town, the route passes the imposing front of the County Gaol **D**, which was built in 1830 to replace the House of Correction. The facade was added to the building in 1865, after the Prison Reform Act, to impress upon would-be offenders the full majesty of the law.

You continue past the school to come to the Church of St Nicholas **E**, whose special features include the nave roof, the screen (partially 15th-century), and the Elizabethan tomb of Richard Herbert. The Robber's Grave in the churchyard is of a John Davies, who was hanged in 1821 as a highwayman. He declared that he was innocent and that no grass would grow on his grave for at least one generation; this proved to be the case.

It is a short walk from the churchyard to the start in Broad Street. If you have time, pay a visit to the Exhibition Centre run by the Civic Society, behind and to the right of the Town Hall in Arthur Street.

JEREMY MOORE

◄*This austere and forbidding facade, which was added to the Georgian County Gaol in 1865, was intended to deter would-be offenders.*

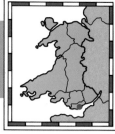

RAY GRANGER. INSET: SORENSEN & OLSEN/NHPA

A Victorian resort, and a country park with an unexpected attraction

Penarth grew up around a tiny church on a headland overlooking Cardiff Bay. In the 19th century, the medieval St Augustine's was replaced by a much grander church, designed by William Butterfield. A fashionable town, home to several ship- and mine-owners, developed on the headland, while a genteel seaside resort grew up southwards along the coast.

A pier ❶ was built there in 1894, and a regular steamship service was established between Clevedon, in Somerset, and Penarth. The pier is still used for steamship sailings today, including the *Waverley*, the last sea-going paddle steamer in the world. It also provides the starting

▲ *The coast path provides sweeping views back to Penarth, dominated by the parish church on Penarth Head. The reed warbler (inset) can be heard in the reed beds at Cosmeston Lakes.*

point for the walk, which soon climbs the hill behind the esplanade, into Windsor Gardens. This strip of lawns and shrubbery, complete with bandstand, was laid out in 1884, and retains an air of quiet gentility.

VIEWS OF SOMERSET

A clifftop path, running first through wide lawns, and then along a gravel track between hedges and fields, gives fine views across the Severn Estuary; beyond the islands of Flat Holm and Steep Holme are Clevedon, Sand Bay and Brean Down, with the Mendips rising

▼ *Near Lavernock, the distinct strata of the cliffs reveal the area's geology.*

behind. Further south are Brent Knoll and the Quantocks.

The coastal path ends, somewhat abruptly, at Lavernock ❷. If the tide allows, you may like to go down to the beach and scramble across the stones to Lavernock Point. From the pavement of limestone beneath the cliffs there are splendid views across the Bristol Channel to Exmoor.

Lavernock today consists of a few

FACT FILE

✴ Penarth, 3 miles (4.8km) south of Cardiff, on the A4160

▭ Pathfinder 1180 (ST 06/16), grid reference ST 189713

miles 0 1 2 3 4 5 6 7 8 9 10 miles
kms 0 1 2 3 4 5 6 7 8 9 10 11 12 13 14 15 kms

◔ Allow 2½ hours

▬ Level walking on good paths and tracks

🅿 Several car parks in Penarth, including a free long-stay car park at the end of Cliff Parade

🍴 Full range of facilities in Penarth. Cafeteria at Cosmeston Lakes Country Park Visitor Centre

ℹ Penarth Tourist Information Centre by the pier has details of the country park's opening times, and of the tours to the medieval village, Tel. (01222) 708849

RAY GRANGER

THE WALK

PENARTH – LAVERNOCK

The walk begins by the pier ⒶⒶ in Penarth.

1 Walk along the front, the sea on your left, to the lifeboat station, about 100 yards (90m) along on your right. Go through the gate and bear left. Climb the iron steps on your right to the roof. Turn left up the concrete steps to Windsor Gardens. Turn left. Continue through the gates and over a crossing path that leads down to the front. At the end of the gardens, bear left around the brick lodge to a road.

2 Cross and turn right to pick up the path running to the left of the shelter. Continue along the clifftop for just over 1½ miles (2.4km), to Lavernock Ⓑ.

3 Turn right past an abandoned farm house and chapel, along a narrow winding road. At a T-junction, cross the busy road with care and climb a gate opposite. Go ahead to the stile opposite. Cosmeston medieval village Ⓒ is on your right.

4 Climb the stile and turn right. The track soon leads between two old quarry pits that are now lakes Ⓓ. Cross a bridge. After 50 paces, turn right and follow the path around the lake to your right. Cosmeston Lakes Country Park Visitor Centre Ⓔ is off to the right. Continue to the main gate.

5 Cross the road and turn left. Take the first right, Cosmeston Drive, and follow it for nearly ¼ mile (400m). About 20 paces beyond Althorp Drive, near the top of a rise, turn left down a gravel track. Continue as this becomes a road. Turn left by the chestnut trees and continue ahead, under the bridge, on the railway path.

6 Where the path opens out into a verge by a road, turn right down Alberta Place. Continue ahead down Alberta Road to a five-way junction. Take the second left, and follow it as it bears left down the seafront to the start.

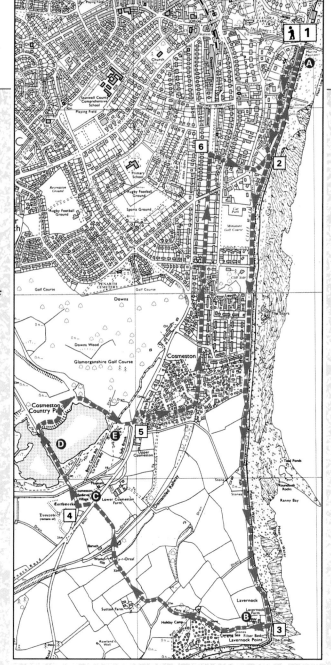

◄ *At Cosmeston, a medieval village is being reconstructed, down to details such as this ancient breed of goat.*

RAY GRANGER

ruined farm buildings and a small church. In the farm, on 11 May 1897, Marconi received the first radio message ever transmitted across water, when his colleague on Flat Holm prosaically asked 'Are you ready?'. A plaque on the churchyard wall commemorates this event.

A lane leads past the chalets of the Marconi Country Club to Cosmeston Ⓒ. This is the site of a village deserted in the 14th century and rediscovered only in 1982. Excavations continue, and the village is slowly being reconstructed on the original foundations using medieval tools, methods and materials.

LAKELAND PARK

The village is within the boundaries of Cosmeston Lakes Country Park, created on the site of some limestone quarries. The route leads along an old lane between the lakes Ⓓ. The one on the right is used for windsurfing and sailing, while that on the left is a conservation area; its islands of reeds and sedges provide nesting places for waterbirds.

The route goes around the pleasure lake and past the visitor centre Ⓔ, which has displays on the park's wildlife, and provides guided tours of the medieval village.

At the main entrance, you cross the main Penarth to Sully road into a modern housing estate built on the site of an old limeworks. A road leads gently uphill to what was once a railway branch line, and is now a footpath leading back into Penarth through the extensive modern development south of the town.

The walk ends with a stroll along the seafront back to the pier. On the way, you pass the ornate Victorian iron verandahs of the Yacht Club and the formal Italian Gardens, which were laid out in 1926.

JASON SMALLEY. INSET: ROY WALLER/NHPA

A walk around Dylan Thomas's home in a sleepy seaside town

▲*Built as a garage for Laugharne's first car, this shed was where Dylan Thomas wrote* **Under Milk Wood.** *It overlooks the Taf Estuary, where the dab (top right) is a common flatfish.*

Laugharne (pronounced Larn) nestles snugly in the folds of the Carmarthenshire hills, overlooking the broad golden sands of the Taf Estuary. During the 16th century, it was the haunt of pirates who preyed on ships in the bustling Bristol Channel. Laugharne was a thriving medieval port; its fabulous Norman castle, built on a site occupied by the last Prince of South Wales, still dominates the ancient town.

Despite its colourful history and intrinsic beauty, Laugharne is better known today as the place where the poet Dylan Thomas spent the last four years of his life. Thomas, whose rich, dense imagery won him early acclaim, is perhaps best remembered for a prose work, the radio play *Under Milk Wood*. It is tempting to see echoes of Llareggub, the play's fictional setting, in Laugharne, though many scholars believe the work was based on Newquay, in Cardiganshire.

FAIRYTALE CASTLE

The walk begins at Laugharne Castle **Ⓐ**, a fairytale ruin with ivy-clad walls studded with blue periwinkles. The site was originally

FACT FILE

- Laugharne, 14 miles (22.5km) south-west of Carmarthen, on the A4066

- Pathfinders 1081 (SN 21/31) and 1105 (SN 20/30), grid reference SN 301107

  miles 0 1 2 3 4 5 6 7 8 9 10 miles
  kms 0 1 2 3 4 5 6 7 8 9 10 11 12 13 14 15 kms

- Allow about 3 hours

- Coastal and woodland paths, farm tracks and tarmac. No steep climbs; suitable for all ages. Some sections may be muddy after rain

- Ⓟ Free parking at the start near Laugharne Castle

- Several pubs in Laugharne

- Restaurants in Laugharne and a tea-room at the Boat House

- The Boat House is open April-October, daily, 10am-5pm, and November-March, daily, 10.30am-3pm

THE WALK

LAUGHARNE CASTLE – ROCHE CASTLE – SIR JOHN'S HILL

The walk begins from the car park near Laugharne Castle Ⓐ *in the centre of the town.*

1 Head towards the water. Cross a footbridge and follow the coastal path below the castle.

2 Fork left up a rocky path leading to some concrete steps. At the top of the steps, bear right past Dylan Thomas's writing shed Ⓑ. Continue on the tarmac path.

3 After about 50 yards (45m), descend some steps to visit the Boat House Ⓒ. Return to the tarmac path and turn right to follow Dylan's Walk Ⓓ into woodland. Cross a tarmac lane and continue along the woodland path, keeping left on the main route at a fork.

4 At a step stile, cross into a field. Follow the line of the hedge to your right. Head for a step stile in the hedgerow behind a tree on the far side of the field. Cross the stile and field towards a farm. Go over a step stile and past a ruined building. Continue through the farmyard to the left of the farmhouse. Go up the farm lane, and continue through a gate.

5 Shortly after a road joins from your right, turn left, then bear right, downhill, on the road.

6 Enter the graveyard of St Martin's Church Ⓔ through a kissing-gate at the end of the stone wall on your right. On the far side of the church are some steps. Bear left over the footbridge into the modern burial ground. Go uphill to pass Dylan Thomas's grave in the centre of the graveyard. Exit through a kissing-gate in the centre of the hedge at the top and turn right along a farm track. Continue downhill to a tarmac road.

7 Turn right. Take the next left to pass Sea View Ⓕ on your right. Turn right into Market Lane. Continue, past the Town Hall Ⓖ on your right, to the main road.

8 Go straight over the crossroads and downhill. Bear right, then turn left over a stone road-bridge. Continue on the road, bearing right onto a main road at The Lacques Ⓗ. At a fork beside a cottage, bear left onto a track. Take a narrow footpath to the right of a house, over a footbridge, and continue to an open field and the site of Roche Castle Ⓙ.

9 Turn left and follow the line of the hedge to a step stile. Cross and go between some buildings to a fork. Bear left to reach a main road. Turn right for about 200 yards (180m), then go sharp left alongside a metal garage onto a waymarked footpath. Continue through the gate. At a second gate, turn right over a stile into a field and go uphill, following the line of the hedge into the next field.

10 After about 30 yards (27m), turn left into the adjacent field. Bear left to follow the line of the hedge around the field, heading for the gated opening in the stone wall opposite. Go through, then diagonally right, heading for a waymarked opening at the top of the field.

11 Cross the stone step stile and follow the path down to the bottom right-hand corner of the field. Continue down the footpath. At a fork, bear left. Continue past a ruin to a T-junction of paths.

12 Turn left and follow the woodland path around Sir John's Hill Ⓚ towards Laugharne. Turn left at a tarmac lane and return to the car park.

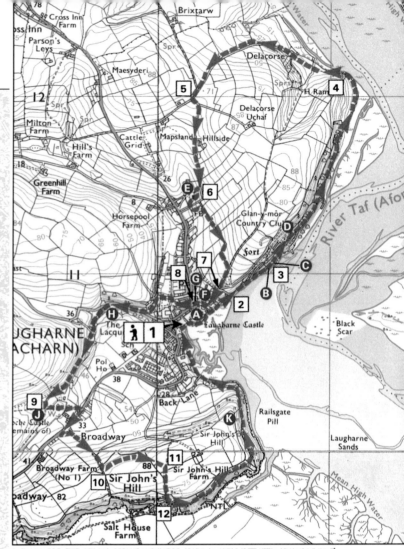

fortified by the Romans, and later by Rhys ap Gruffydd, who was the last Prince of South Wales.

Laugharne Castle was captured twice by the Welsh in the 13th century, and was remodelled, with Tudor embellishments, at the close of the 16th century by Sir John Perrot, High Admiral and reputed half-brother of Queen Elizabeth I. In the Civil War, the Royalist castle was destroyed by Cromwell's forces.

Just beyond the castle, looking out across the broad estuary, is an inconspicuous wooden shed Ⓑ. This belongs to the Boat House, and was built out over the cliff-edge on stilts in the early 1900s. The shack was the garage of the first-ever motor vehicle to be seen in Laugharne. The car terrorized the local draught horses and convinced at least one inhabitant that Satan himself had come. Undeterred, she armed herself with a pitchfork and charged off in pursuit of the green Wolseley.

In the late spring of 1949, Mrs Margaret Taylor, Dylan Thomas's generous patroness, purchased the house and the poet turned the garage into his 'workshack'. A damp, draughty, overgrown place, it was hardly comfortable, but it was

◄*Laugharne Castle, once painted by Turner, has two 13th-century towers. The interior of Thomas's workshack (above) gives the impression that the writer has just slipped out to the pub.*

the path. Near the shoreline stands a more ominous ruin, known as Burnt House. According to local legend, it was deliberately destroyed after a murder was committed there.

The walk through the shady graveyard of St Martin's Church ❺ winds beneath a canopy of venerable yews through a tangle of vegetation, crumbling gravestones and fallen angels. The beautiful church, which dates from the 14th century, is one of the earliest in the area. It was probably built by Sir Guy de Brian, Edward III's Lord High Admiral. The path crosses a bridge to a modern burial

peaceful. 'You have given me life', wrote Thomas to Mrs Taylor, 'and now I am going to live it'.

The path leads down to the Boat House ❸, which Thomas called 'my sea-shaken house on a breakneck of rocks', a three-storey cottage tucked into the base of red sandstone cliffs. After the poet's premature death, the house stood empty for many years until 1975, when it was opened as a memorial to him.

DYLAN'S WALK

The route continues along Dylan's Walk ❹. Originally known as Cliff Walk, it was renamed in 1958, the year *Under Milk Wood* was first performed in Laugharne. Across the 'dab-filled bay' to your right are the fertile, checkerboard hills of Carmarthenshire. The ivy-choked remains of cottages are scattered through the wood along the side of

◄ *The Boat House, bought for Dylan Thomas by Margaret Taylor, wife of the late historian A J P Taylor, is now a museum to the poet. Parts of the old town, such as Market Lane (right), are little changed.*

Dylan Thomas

▲*The Town Hall's clock tower inspired an image in* Under Milk Wood.

Augustus John's portrait of Dylan Thomas hangs in the National Museum in Cardiff.

The son of an English teacher and a farmer's daughter, Dylan Thomas was born in Swansea in 1914. From his parents, he imbibed a fascination for language — his father read him Shakespeare as bedtime stories — and a love of the Welsh countryside; his visits to his maternal grandparents' farm are fondly remembered in his poem *Fern Hill*.

He was a prolific writer in his adolescence, and published his first volume, *18 Poems*, in 1934. Most of the lyrical, Romantic poems he wrote existed, at least in embryo form, before he moved to London in 1935. He married in 1936, and for the rest of his life he struggled to support his growing family and his fondness for socializing.

In 1949, he moved to Laugharne, where he worked intensely in his 'water and tree room on the cliff' or slipped quietly away along the cliff path for a relaxing drink at Brown's Hotel. During this period he wrote *Under Milk Wood*, but composed little published poetry.

Reading tours of the United States offered him a financial lifeline — he was deeply in debt to his friends and to the Inland Revenue. He found the tours exhausting, not least because he was continually plied with whisky. Though Thomas liked to drink, he had no head for strong liquor and kept to beer when he was at home in Wales.

His fourth tour of the States, in November 1953, was intended to take him to California, and a meeting with Igor Stravinsky, with whom he hoped to create an opera. However, after a reception in New York, he fell into a coma and died. The verdict of the doctor who wrote the death certificate, that the 39-year-old poet died of an 'insult to the brain', left open the question of whether an overdose of alcohol had killed him, or whether it was a mixture of drink and medicines.

when Myfanwy Price dreams of 'her lover, tall as the town clock-tower'.

Further on, the narrow lane ❶ that winds along the banks of a murmuring stream has the curious name, The Lacques, which means a moist or splashy place. At one time, there were several wells here, rising from springs beneath the tree-lined banks. These springs were much frequented during the Victorian era, when the water was credited with remarkable restorative powers.

ROCHE CASTLE

Trees and overgrown hedgerows give way to open farmland and the site of Roche Castle ❶, which according to local stories has a subterranean tunnel connecting it with Laugharne Castle. It fell into disrepair, and masonry was taken to build new houses at Broadway; the ancient stones can be seen in buildings near the road. The local inhabitants of Laugharne used to gather among the ruins of Roche Castle, which was once owned by the Perrot family, to play bowls, dance and watch cockfights.

WILD FLOWERS

The walk continues up through sloping fields, then passes through mature woods. Wall pennywort, red campion, hart's tongue fern, cuckoo pint, wood anemone, ragged robin and delicate spotted orchid crowd the edges of the narrow path.

The return track leaves Sir John's Hill ❶, where Sir John Perrot planned to build a house to watch the activities of the pirates. This hill can be seen from Dylan Thomas's own window, and it inspired him to write his first poem from the work-shack, a musing on mortality that begins, 'Over Sir John's Hill
The hawk on fire hangs still'.

▼*Curving between low hills, the broad estuary of the Afon Taf is spectacular whether the tide is low, as here, or high.*

ground, the final resting place of Dylan Thomas. His simple, white wooden cross contrasts sharply with the grander headstones made of carved marble that surround it.

As you return through the town, the route passes Sea View ❶, a simplistic doll's house of a building, its three storeys of rooms piled neatly on top of one another. Thomas lived here for some time with his wife, Caitlin, and their children.

FAMOUS CLOCK

As you cross King Street, the Town Hall and jail ❶ is to your right. A building of considerable antiquity, it was rebuilt in 1745. Its white clock tower features in *Under Milk Wood*,

INDEX

Index compiled by INDEXING SPECIALISTS, Hove